A HISTORY OF
MULTICULTURAL AMERICA

The Civil War to the Last Frontier
1850-1880s

William Loren Katz

RSVP
**RAINTREE
STECK-VAUGHN**
P U B L I S H E R S
The Steck-Vaughn Company

Austin, Texas

For Laurie

Cover and interior design: Joyce Spicer
Electronic production: Scott Melcer

Library of Congress Cataloging-in-Publication Data

Katz, William Loren.
    The Civil War to the last frontier, 1850-1880s / by William Loren Katz.
        p.   cm. — (A History of multicultural America)
    Includes index.
    Summary: A multicultural history of the United States, from 1850-1880, focussing on the events before, during, and after the Civil War and discussing the experiences of various ethnic groups, notably blacks, Native Americans, and Chinese immigrants, during this period.
    ISBN 0-8114-6277-3   —   ISBN 0-8114-2914-8 (softcover)
    1. United States — History — 1849-1877 — Juvenile literature.
[1. United States — History — 1849-1877]   I. Title.   II. Series: Katz, William Loren. History of multicultural America.
E415.7.K38   1993
973.5—dc20   92-17924
                                                              CIP
                                                               AC

Printed and bound in the United States of America

1 2 3 4 5 6 7 8 9 0 LB 98 97 96 95 94 93

Acknowledgments

All prints from the collection of the author, William L. Katz.

Cover photographs: (inset) The Granger Collection; (map) North Wind Picture Archive

TABLE OF CONTENTS

INTRODUCTION

The history of the United States is the story of people of many backgrounds. A few became wealthy through their knowledge of science, industry, or banking. But it was ordinary people who most shaped the progress of this country and created our national heritage.

The American experience, however, has often been recounted in history books as the saga of powerful men—presidents and senators, merchants and industrialists. Schoolchildren were taught that the wisdom and patriotism of an elite created democracy and prosperity.

A truthful history of the United States has to do more than celebrate the contributions of the few. Ordinary Americans fought the Revolution that set this country free, and ordinary workers built the nation's economy. The overwhelming majority of people held no office, made little money, and worked hard all their lives.

Some groups, women and minorities in particular, had to vault legal barriers and public hostility in order to make their contributions to the American dream, only to find that school courses taught little about their achievements. The valiant struggle of minorities and women to win dignity, equality, and justice often was omitted from history's account. Some believe this omission was accidental or careless, others insist it was purposeful.

Native Americans struggled valiantly to survive military and cultural assaults on their lives. But the public was told Native Americans were savages undeserving of any rights to their land or culture. African Americans battled to break the chains of slavery and to scale the walls of racial discrimination. But a century after slavery ended, some textbooks still pictured African Americans as content under slavery and bewildered by freedom. Arrivals from Asia, Mexico, and the West Indies faced legal restrictions and sometimes violence. But the public was told that they were undeserving of a welcome because they took "American jobs," and some were "treacherous aliens."

Whether single, married, or mothers, women were portrayed as dependent on men and accepting of a lowly status. The record of their sturdy labors, enduring strengths, and their arduous struggle to achieve equality rarely found its way into classrooms. The version of American history that reached the public carried many prejudices. It often preferred farmers over urban workers, middle classes over working classes, rich over poor. Women and minorities became invisible, ineffective, or voiceless.

This distorted legacy also failed to mention the campaigns waged by minorities and women to attain human rights. Such efforts did not reflect glory on white male rulers and their unwillingness to extend democracy and opportunity to others.

This kind of history was not a trustworthy tale. It locked out entire races and impeded racial understanding. Not only was it unreliable, but for most students it was dull and boring.

Our history has to be truthful and complete. Our struggle to overcome the barriers of nature and obstacles made by humans is an inspiring story. This series of books seeks to explore the heroic efforts of minorities and women to find their place in the American dream.

William Loren Katz

CHAPTER 1

MARCHING TO WAR: THE 1850s

During the 1850s Americans were increasingly forced to deal with the issue of slavery. The country was divided between states where slavery had been abolished and states where slavery was still practiced. Trouble escalated when Congress passed the Compromise of 1850, which included a new Fugitive Slave Law that allowed federal officials to force ordinary citizens to assist in catching runaway slaves. Anyone who refused to help slave-hunting posses or who aided the fugitives faced heavy fines and imprisonment. Northerners reacted angrily. To exempt their citizens from the law's demands, many states passed personal liberty laws. Passions rose sharply. In Ohio the gentle Quakers announced, "WE GO FOR REVOLUTION!" And more whites than ever were willing to aid slaves who escaped and to defy the slave-hunters.

African Americans prepared for battle. Lewis Hayden, an ex-slave who lived in Boston, placed two kegs of explosives in his cellar and dared anyone to enter his home searching for runaways. Black editor Martin Delany warned that any U.S. official, from a sheriff to the president, who entered his house looking for runaways would leave a corpse.

In September 1851, in Christiana, Pennsylvania, fugitive slave William Parker armed and trained a small army of African

This poster in Boston warned black people to beware of slave-catchers from the south.

In 1851 William Parker and his armed fugitive slaves drove off a posse of slave-catchers led by a U.S. marshal.

American men to confront slave-hunters. When a Federal posse rode in to arrest two runaways hiding in Parker's house, there was a gunfight. After the smoke cleared, a slave master lay dead and his son was wounded. Federal authorities sent 45 Marines to Christiana. Two Quakers and 36 Blacks were tried for treason and found not guilty. With aid from Frederick Douglass, Parker, his followers, and the runaways reached Canada. "The only way to meet the man-hunter successfully is with cold steel and the nerve to use it," said Douglass. He later called Christiana the first shot of the Civil War.

From the eastern seaboard to the Middle West, Blacks and whites in the North formed vigilance committees to challenge slave-hunting posses. Seizure of runaways led to riots and shoot-outs. When slave Anthony Burns was arrested in Boston in 1854, it took 22 military units to hold back crowds and return Burns to slavery.

Thomas Garrett

The struggle over whether Kansas would become a free or a slave state led to a small civil war. Slaveholders sent in armed men who clashed with free-state supporters. Fiery John Brown assembled a band that included Europeans, African Americans, and his five sons to combat the pro-slavery forces in Kansas.

The Underground Railroad accelerated its activities. In Delaware runaways were aided by Samuel Burris, a young African American, and Thomas Garrett, an elderly Quaker. Burris was captured and auctioned as a slave. But the highest bidder had been secretly sent by Garrett to buy Burris and set him free.

Garrett was one of many whites who made great personal sacrifices in their struggle against slavery. He had to pay a fortune in court fines. Out of money, he still told a judge, "If anyone knows of a fugitive who wants shelter, and a friend, *send him to Thomas Garrett.*"

Samuel Burris

Many immigrants, particularly those who had fled tyranny in Europe, became early supporters of the Free Soil Party and then the Republican Party because both opposed slavery's extension. In 1847 Norwegian Americans published their first paper, *Northern Lights*. It proudly reprinted the Declaration of Independence and announced its support for the principles of the Free Soil Party.

In 1848 the first Jewish American weekly paper appeared in New York City. Its publisher, Isador Bush, later went to Missouri where he spoke not only against slavery extension but also for immediate emancipation.

White abolitionists suffered for their views. In Illinois anti-slavery editor Elijah Lovejoy was slain by a mob as he defended his printing press. In 1851 Norwegian immigrant and abolitionist Elsie Warnskjold confronted fellow Texans over slavery. Years later her husband was assassinated for supporting the Union.

David Broderick lost his life in the struggle against slavery. Born in Ireland, Broderick arrived in California as a 49er. He entered politics as a Democrat and in 1857 was elected to the United States Senate. He threw himself into the fight to prevent owners of slaves from controlling his party or his adopted homeland.

After firing into the ground in a duel, Senator David Broderick is slain by Chief Justice Terry, his pro-slavery opponent.

Broderick's views soon collided with the pro-slavery stand of his party and with the administration of Democratic President James Buchanan. During Broderick's 1859 election campaign the pro-slavery Chief Justice of California's Supreme Court challenged the Senator to a duel. Broderick felt he could not ignore the dare, but did not wish to hurt anyone. The two men faced each other with pistols, and Broderick fired into the ground. His foe took careful aim and shot him in the heart.

Immigrants who resided in the South found it easier and safer not to criticize slavery, which was an institution protected by the state. Still, many foreigners in the South did become an antislavery force. The 35,000 German Americans in Texas were one-sixth of the state's population, and when *New York Times* reporter Frederick Olmsted toured the state in the 1850s he did not find one German American who owned a slave. The settlers loved to reason, argue, and to display their lack of prejudices, Olmsted found. Fearing for their safety, they did not challenge slaveholders in loud voices or in print, but undermined slavery in small ways. Slave owners saw these new citizens as a disturbing presence in their controlled society.

Some members of minority groups dared to speak out about slavery. Czech Americans in St. Louis and Texas published antislavery papers. In 1851 antislavery German Americans in Richmond, Virginia, started a Social Democratic Association that opposed bondage. In Baltimore, arrivals from Germany launched a paper, *Der Wecker,* to denounce slavery. When *Der Wecker's* editor died, his widow continued the publication. In 1854 antislavery German Americans issued Louisville's *Herold de Westens.*

While most leading U.S. religious denominations tried to steer clear of the slavery controversy, some clergymen did speak out against slavery. From his pulpit at Har Sinai Temple in Baltimore, Rabbi David Einhorn, who migrated from Austria in 1855, cited the Bible in his sermons opposing slavery. The chains on Africans, the rabbi insisted, threatened liberty for all. By 1861 his daring stand forced Rabbi Einhorn to flee Maryland, a slave state, for the North.

Many immigrants had initially been supporters of the Democratic Party forged earlier in the 1800s by President Andrew Jackson because he had championed the "age of the common man." But in the conflict over slavery, immigrants began to desert the Democratic Party, which had come under the control of slaveholders. In 1851 a "Swedish American Republican Club of Illinois" was started. The next year the "Democratic Society of Polish Refugees" began by organizing a plan for Poland's independence from Russia, but it ended up denouncing slavery.

European refugees took a leading role in protesting the Kansas-Nebraska Act that in 1854 opened new western lands to slavery. German Americans and others held large protest meetings in Chicago, Galveston, Cincinnati, Buffalo, Louisville, and other cities.

In December 1854, Adolph Douai, a German political exile and editor of the San Antonio *Zeitung,* published a strong attack on slavery. The Austin *State Times* then urged its readers to throw Douai's printing press into the San Antonio River.

In 1856, as conflict in Kansas turned violent, immigrant laborers increasingly left the Democratic Party for the Republican Party and its presidential candidate, John Charles Fremont. Republican Party officials began a concerted effort to win German and other immigrant voters in Iowa, Ohio, and Wisconsin.

In a Kansas aflame over the slavery issue, abolitionist John Brown recruited two Jewish immigrants into his band, Austrian American August Bondi and Polish American Theodore Weiner. By 1859, another Jewish immigrant, Moritz Pinner, was publishing the antislavery *Kansas Post.*

Pathfinder John Charles Fremont, of French descent, was the new Republican Party's first presidential candidate.

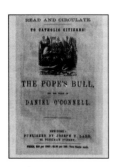

Irish American appeal to vote against slavery in 1856.

The war between pro- and antislavery forces in Kansas sparked resistance by the enslaved throughout the South. In 1856 a Kansas journalist reported, "The slaves are in a state of insurrection all over the country." In Colorado County, Texas, a paper revealed that 200 rebel slaves were being helped by "the Mexican population."

Black women played a leading part in the rising opposition to slavery in the South. In the 1850s Harriet Tubman led 300 slaves out of bondage in Maryland, and in Kentucky Jane Lewis eluded slave-hunting posses to help fugitives reach free soil. Some conductors of the Underground Railroad brought their passengers to former slave Arnold Cragston, who in four years rowed hundreds of runaways across the Ohio River. He said, "We just knew there was a lot of slaves always a-wantin' to get free, and I had to help 'em."

Immigrant workers who were not abolitionists had reason to fear the slaveholder power. For foreigners the public schools fulfilled the great promise of America's opportunities. But slaveholders firmly opposed public education as "dangerous to stability" and the "worst of abominations."

For the North and South, the division over slavery reached a turning point in 1859 when John Brown led a raid on Harper's Ferry, a small town in what is now West Virginia. Brown's small band included among others his own sons and five African American volunteers. They intended to arm slaves and help them establish colonies in the nearby mountains from which guerrilla raids would be launched against the slave system. Brown's effort failed, and his men were trapped and either slain or captured.

John Brown (right) and his band at Harper's Ferry.

Most white Northerners did not approve of John Brown's raid. But they agreed that Brown had looked at slavery and declared that the time of day was high noon. German Americans held a meeting in Cincinnati and announced that Brown "has powerfully contributed to bring out the hidden consciousness of the majority of the people." African American men and women welcomed his blow against a system that held them in chains.

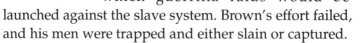

Osborne Perry Anderson was one of five African Americans who fought with John Brown at Harper's Ferry.

C H A P T E R   2

THE ELECTION OF 1860 AND SECESSION

American minorities played a crucial role in the election of Abraham Lincoln to the presidency and in the war crisis that followed. Republican Party officials carefully courted immigrant voters. Long before he entered the presidential race, Lincoln owned a German-language newspaper and tried to master German grammar. In 1855 his scathing attack on the Know-Nothings made him a favorite among foreign-born voters. To Swedish American laborers, Lincoln was *arbetaresonen*, or "son of the working man."

At the time of the 1860 election there were some 700,000 German Americans in the United States. Their votes could mean victory or defeat for Republicans in Missouri, Iowa, Illinois, Indiana, Wisconsin, Ohio, Minnesota, Michigan, Maryland, New York, Pennsylvania, New Jersey, Connecticut, and possibly California and Massachusetts.

At the 1860 nominating convention in Chicago, Republican delegates adopted proposals submitted by a conference of German Americans. These "German planks" favored a homestead law and political equality for foreign-born Americans.

Lincoln's record attracted immigrants. A poor, self-educated man, Lincoln had become a lawyer and a politician. To newly arrived Europeans, Lincoln embodied America's opportunities for success. Although not an abolitionist, he was committed to rule by small farmers rather than slaveholders in the western territories. He had not been afraid to speak out against slavery and he denounced prejudice against foreigners.

Abraham Lincoln

Jewish Americans welcomed Lincoln's rejection of bigotry and his personal friendship with Abraham Jonas. After Lincoln became President, he appointed Jonas the postmaster of Quincy, Illinois.

In their effort to carry the election campaign into immigrant communities, the Republican Party signed up key foreign-language speakers. Carl Schurz traveled 21,000 miles promoting Lincoln and the Republicans. Hungarian American Julian Kune campaigned for the Party throughout Indiana. Both foreign-born men advanced Lincoln's nomination at the Republican national convention.

As Election Day neared, Republican support grew among the foreign-born. German and Scandinavian American workers held pro-Lincoln rallies in major cities from St. Louis to New York. A Republican paper thanked them for their "zeal and energy."

Abolitionist meetings, such as this one in 1860, were often attacked by pro-slavery mobs. Black leader Frederick Douglass is shown trying to finish his speech.

Most Irish American voters traditionally had favored the Democratic Party because it usually had welcomed immigrants. But some Irish Americans broke away from the party to organize Lincoln rallies in Boston, Philadelphia, and New York. One speaker said that in the past the Democrats spoke for the rights of workers "and particularly those of foreign birth," but it no longer did so. A vote for Lincoln and his Homestead Bill, he said, would make farms available for the poor and thus would also reduce competition for city jobs.

"If Lincoln is elected, you will have to compete with the labor of four million emancipated Negroes," answered the Democratic New York *Herald* in an appeal circulated to Irish and German American laborers the week before men trooped to the polls.

Pressure increased with the approach of the fateful day. In Brooklyn, German American clothing workers were called together by employers and told their jobs depended on a Democratic victory. But abolitionist and German immigrant Joseph Wedemeyer spoke up to urge a vote for the Republicans. Others then rose to echo his political views. Republican papers called on immigrant voters for support on Election Day. "German fellow-citizens, be on your guard. Stand firm for Lincoln and Liberty," urged the New York *Tribune*.

The election found immigrants, like other Americans, were divided but most voted for Lincoln and the Republicans. Upon Lincoln's election, 11 Southern states seceded from the Union and formed the Confederate States of America. The secession crisis further divided minorities, as it did other Americans.

In the South, the new Confederacy sought unity but found its recent immigrants were often a thorn in its side. In Missouri pro-Union German Americans helped neutralize that key state. Using an illegally recruited and armed German American militia force, Republican politicians seized St. Louis' arsenal. General Franz Sigel, a German refugee, and his German American troops held Missouri for a crucial ten months and set the stage for later Union military victories. In Texas, a company of German Americans stirred Confederate anxiety when it refused to surrender its Union flag. The soldiers were promptly disbanded.

CHAPTER 3

THE CIVIL WAR AND NATIVE AMERICANS

The Civil War years were difficult for Native Americans. Many lived on reservations but the rights to their lands were often violated. The Santee Sioux had to contend with Minnesota pioneers who defied treaties to settle on Sioux land. Cheated out of their food by U.S. Indian agents, the Sioux also faced starvation. Chief Big Eagle, a Sioux leader, later recalled the basic cause of friction:

> The whites are always trying to make the Indians give up their life and live like white men — go to farming, work hard and do as they do.... If the Indians had tried to make whites live like them, the whites would have resisted, and it was the same way with many Indians.

In the summer of 1862 starving Sioux heard a trader say, "If they are hungry, let them eat grass or their own dung." The Sioux decided to fight back, and rampages took innocent lives on both sides.

One Sioux leader, Chief Little Crow, led his followers from Minnesota, but U.S. troops rounded up the Santee Sioux who had not taken part in the war and hundreds were sentenced to death. President Lincoln commuted the death sentences of all but 38. Some

The mass execution of 38 Sioux men in Mankato, Minnesota.

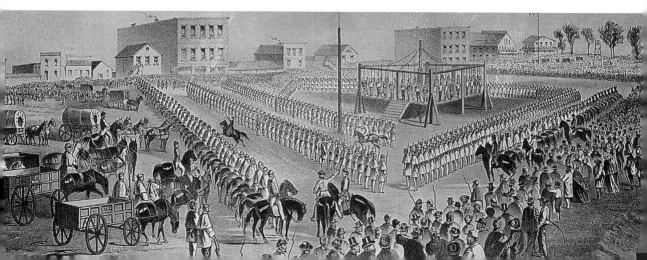

of these were not guilty of any crime, and one had risked his life to save a white family. The hanging of the 38 Sioux on one scaffold was the largest execution in U.S. history.

The United States then claimed that the aggression of the Sioux gave Washington the right to violate its treaties with the Santee. Whites seized Sioux lands in Minnesota and the Sioux nation was settled on barren land. A third of the Sioux died the first winter.

In Arizona and New Mexico in 1862, the United States continued its effort to eliminate the powerful Apache nation. But under Geronimo, Nana, Cochise, and Victorio, Apaches had become skilled fighters. Still, in 1864 scout Kit Carson led 8,000 Apaches on a "March of Tears" to Fort Sumner, New Mexico, and held them captive for five years.

The U.S. also struck at Native Americans in Colorado. In 1861, 38 of 44 leaders of the Cheyenne and Arapaho rejected a U.S. invitation to a peace council. Saying the others could sign later, the United States negotiated a treaty with the six people who attended. None of the absent ever signed, yet the government said the agreement was binding on all. Then even the signers found they had been tricked. They had surrendered most of their land and were not allowed hunting rights. Next white squatters arrived with U.S. troops as protection.

In 1864 John Evans, Governor of the Colorado Territory, declared any Cheyennes leaving the reservation would be treated as enemies. The Colorado militia of 700 men, led by Colonel James Chivington, came upon a sleeping Cheyenne village at Sand Creek and opened fire with their rifles and four howitzers. Cheyenne survivors joined the Sioux nation and carried out retaliation raids the next year.

For Native Americans confined to reservations in the Oklahoma Indian Territory, the Civil War brought tragedy. In 1861, the Confederate States flooded the Indian Territory with its agents. Pressure mounted and many Native American leaders felt they had no choice but to ally their nations with the Confederacy.

Opothle Yahola, a Creek Chief, then gathered African and Native Americans who were neutral or favored the Union. Seminoles, Creeks, and other Indians rushed to his camp. He wrote to Lincoln offering loyalty and peace, and asking for protection:

...now the wolf has come. Men who are strangers tread our soil. Our children are frightened & mothers cannot sleep for fear.

Confederate armies raced after Yahola's families. The Creek leader and his followers were mauled again and again as they tried to reach safety. A Seminole reported the carnage:

...we lost everything we possessed, everything to take care of our women and children with, and all that we had.... We left them in cold blood by the wayside.

Desperate, Yahola led his people toward Kansas where they finally reached the Union lines. By April 1862, most of the surviving men in his band enlisted in the Union cause under Senator Jim Lane. Yahola's soldiers proved among the toughest sent into battle as Lane led them on raids into Missouri that freed slaves. Men that Lane had recruited from Opothle Yahola's forces thus took part in some of the earliest battles of the war and were among the first United States troops to free enslaved people.

Senator Jim Lane (center) led his Indian troops on raids into Missouri.

THE CIVIL WAR

For minorities, as for other Americans, the Civil War was an opportunity to prove their valor and loyalty. When Lincoln issued his first call for volunteers in April 1861, the foreign-born rushed to the colors. Among the first mustered into the Union Army were a De Kalb regiment of German American clerks, the Garibaldi Guards made up of Italian Americans, a "Polish Legion," and hundreds of Irish American youths from Boston and New York. But in Ohio and Washington, D.C., African American volunteers were turned away from recruiting stations and told, "This is a white man's war."

Prominent immigrant leaders in trade unions were among the earliest volunteers. John Farquahr, born in Scotland and president of the National Typographical Union, enlisted as a private in the 89th Illinois Regiment. He rose to become a major and after the war served as a congressman. Joseph Wedemeyer was one of thousands of German Americans who rushed to enlist in the Army.

The German American 7th (Steuben) Regiment of 850 assembles before City Hall, New York City, to receive their regimental banner from Miss Bertha Kapff, daughter of their Lt. Colonel.

Some citizens questioned the loyalty of immigrants who lived in crowded city tenements until an Italian American from Brooklyn turned that around. In the New York Senate, Democrat Francis Spinola had been a vigorous foe of Republican policies and Lincoln. But now he swore his loyalty with stirring words, "This is my flag, which I will follow and defend." His speech, said a congressman, "gave assurance that the masses in the great cities were devoted to the Union and ready to enlist for its defense." In 1863 President Lincoln appointed Spinola a brigadier general. Spinola was twice wounded leading his brigade in bayonet charges.

More than 440,000 European immigrants fought for the Union, including more than 170,000 Germans and more than 150,000 Irish.

Many saw their service as a proud sacrifice. "I have lived solely for the future of my fatherland, and I fought for America, looking death boldly in the face tens of times, as becomes a Pole," wrote Captain Louis Zychlinski.

August Bondi, a Jewish immigrant from Poland who rode with John Brown in Kansas, enlisted in the 5th Kansas Cavalry Regiment. He was wounded he said, defending "equal rights to all beliefs." At 70, Bondi still wrote passionately about his life of action:

> I do not regret a single step or instance in my long life to further and assist the realization of my devout wishes that tyranny and despotism may perish, and bigotry and fanaticism may be wiped from the face of the earth.

The first officer to die for the Union was Captain Constatin Blandowski, one of many immigrants who earlier had fought for freedom in Europe and then joined Lincoln's army. Born in Upper Silesia and trained at Dresden, Germany, he was a veteran of democratic struggles — a Polish revolt at Krakow, the Polish Legion's battles against Austria, and the Hungarian fight for independence.

Blandowski responded to Lincoln's first call for volunteers and joined General Franz Sigel's 3rd Missouri Volunteers. During the siege of Camp Jackson, near St. Louis, less than a month after the assault on Fort Sumter, he was wounded and later died from his injuries.

Out of a total population of 7,000 Swedish American men, 1,300 volunteered. Entire units from Iowa, Wisconsin, Minnesota, and Illinois were comprised of Swedish Americans. In Stockholm, Sweden, 2,000 men wished to volunteer for the Union Army.

General Franz Sigel and his troops helped keep Missouri loyal to the Union.

Some immigrants chose to serve in units with men who spoke their language. In Wisconsin the 9th Regiment was German American, the 15th Regiment was Scandinavian American, and the 17th Regiment was Irish American. In Iowa's 22nd Regiment and Wisconsin's 36th, Czech Americans made up entire companies.

But most foreigners chose to serve in English-speaking units. Michigan troops, for example, marched into battle with 420 Dutch

Americans. Lithuanian Americans contributed five officers and 373 enlisted men sprinkled throughout Lincoln's armed forces. New York regiments represented a mixture of immigrant groups. Czech Americans, for example, served in six New York regiments.

From New York alone 100 Italian Americans became Union officers. Enrico Fardella arrived from Italy in 1860 and soon became a colonel. After he displayed his heroism at the Battle of Plymouth, North Carolina, he was made a brigadier general. General Stephen Kearny called Fardella "a noble and brave old soldier. His only difficulty is that he does not speak English fluently."

The Medal of Honor was first awarded during the Civil War.

Some immigrants earned the Congressional Medal of Honor. Italian American officer Louis di Cesnola, was the Colonel of the 4th Cavalry Regiment. At Aldie, Virginia, in 1863, he earned the Medal of Honor and was appointed a general. He charged unarmed at the foe, read his citation, "rallied his men ...until desperately wounded and taken prisoner in action." In 1879 Cesnola became director of New York's Metropolitan Museum of Art. The museum then became, wrote a critic, "a monument to his energy, enterprise, and rare executive skill."

Italian American privates also won the Medal of Honor. Joseph Sova of the 8th Cavalry earned it for capturing the Confederate flag

The 39th New York Infantry, the Garibaldi Guards, were mostly recent immigrants from Italy and also included men from Ireland, Scotland, and Germany.

at Appomattox. Private Orlando Caruana of the 51st Infantry won it at Newburn, North Carolina. With bullets whizzing past him, he saved wounded men and rescued the U.S. flag.

Some immigrant soldiers were remembered fondly by their comrades. Polish American Gustav Magnitsky answered Lincoln's first call for volunteers and served as a sergeant under Captain (later Supreme Court Justice) Oliver Wendell Holmes, who commanded the 20th Massachusetts Regiment at Gettysburg and Petersburg. Holmes remembered Magnitsky as a soldier who had enlisted on principle and was "quiet and steady under fire, quiet and effective in camp, modest, distinguished in bearing and soul." Justice Holmes left this description of his sergeant:

> We had many a heartbreaking march and were in many a battle together and his gallantry and efficiency gained him a commission in a regiment in which a sergeant had to be a fighting man to keep his chevrons and an unusual man to gain the shoulderstraps. He became a captain and in some of the fierce days at the end of the war had the regiment under his command.

Some nationalities contributed more than their share of Union soldiers. The 800 Hungarian American volunteers made them the highest (20%) among any ethnic group. About 100 served as officers, including seven generals, 15 colonels, two lieutenant colonels, 14 majors, and 15 captains.

Many exiles from Hungary had gained military training by fighting Austrian despotism. General Julius H. Stahel was a Hungarian refugee whose first American jobs were as a bookseller and a journalist. By having his men stand their ground at the First Battle of Bull Run, he kept the rout of the Union forces from being a total disaster. Later, Stahel was wounded in a cavalry charge and awarded the Congressional Medal of Honor for his bravery.

General Albin Schoepf was a Hungarian revolutionary whom the Austrians expelled to Turkey. When he arrived in the United States in 1851, he took a porter's job. General Schoepf tried hard to bring a European style of discipline to the Union Army.

Patriotism motivated some immigrants to recruit their own regiments. In Chicago, Geza Mihaloczy first turned to his fellow

Hungarian Americans and then to Slavs and Bohemians for his "Lincoln Riflemen." He received the President's permission to name the regiment after him. When the Lincoln Riflemen merged with the 24th Illinois Infantry Regiment, Mihaloczy became a colonel. He was fatally wounded at the Battle of Chattanooga.

In the West, General John C. Fremont added Brigadier General Alexander Asboth, a Hungarian American, to his staff. Asboth fought bravely in Missouri, and in Arkansas, where he was wounded. He was wounded twice again in Florida. Asboth survived to be appointed later American Minister to Argentina. Another of Fremont officer's, Captain Nicolae Dunca, a Romanian American, died fighting with the 9th New York Regiment in Virginia.

Not all Hungarian American officers were Christians. General Frederick Knefler had been a Jewish carpenter in Hungary. In America he had studied law. Another Hungarian refugee, Major Charles Zagony, had become a Muslim when he was in Turkey. His first American job was as a house painter. When the war started, Zagony organized trappers, hunters, and pioneers into three companies. He not only recruited "Fremont's Body Guards" but also designed their uniforms, using bright Hungarian military outfits as his models. The Major became famous for "Zagony's Death Ride." First he told his men the odds, then led 300 men against a force of almost 2,000 Confederates and they successfully routed the enemy. General Fremont called his act a daring moment in world military history.

Out of a Polish American population of 30,000, more than 4,000 men volunteered. Some were recruited by stirring appeals:

Rally around our banner, under the wing of the Polish
white eagle. The spirit of Pulaski and Kosciusko will
sustain us.

Polish Americans were scattered throughout six New York regiments, two Ohio regiments, two Illinois regiments, and Wisconsin's 26th Regiment. The 58th New York Infantry was sometimes called the "Polish Legion."

About 165 Polish Americans became officers. One of the most daring Union cavalry officers, General Joseph Karge, led a New Jersey cavalry regiment and rode with the famous Grierson's raiders

Krzyzanowski the Liberator

One of the most heroic Civil War soldiers was Wladimir Krzyzanowski, a cousin of composer Frederick Chopin. A student in Poznan, Poland, he reacted so strongly against Russian domination of his homeland that he had to flee. In the United States he helped build railroads and became an abolitionist and a Republican.

Young Krzyzanowski volunteered as a private in the Union Army, recruited a militia company in Washington, D.C., and became a Major in "the Polish Legion." In Virginia his bravery helped stop Stonewall Jackson from decimating Fremont's army. In eight hours of fighting that preceded Bull Run, General Carl Schurz reported that Krzyzanowski "contested every inch of ground against the heavy pressure of a greatly superior force." A horse was shot from under Krzyzanowski but his daring continued to inspire his besieged men.

Lincoln promoted Krzyzanowski to Brigadier General, but the Senate refused to confirm him because, said Schurz, "nobody there could pronounce his name." Krzyzanowski showed no anger and wrote in his *Memoirs*, "A son of a foreign and far off land, I fought for the ideals for freedom and liberty." Though not a general, the intrepid Polish American was handed the command of five regiments in 1863 at Chancellorsville.

At Gettysburg, Krzyzanowski's forces occupied the pivotal position at Cemetery Ridge and held it for days under heavy bombardment. They also saved a battery from capture. Again he was singled out for "bravery, faithfulness and efficiency."

On July 3, during the third and last day of fighting at Gettysburg, came the famous Confederate attack called Pickett's Charge. It was met with withering rifle and cannon fire from Krzyzanowski's position and thrown back. This has been called the decisive Union victory of the war.

Krzyzanowski went on to fight at Chattanooga, at Missionary Ridge, at Knoxville, and for the Army of the Cumberland. He trained six companies from Michigan, Ohio, and Wisconsin.

Throughout his military service Krzyzanowski shared danger, hunger, and exhaustion with his men. In the end they presented him with an engraved sword with the names and dates of his battles. In 1938, his remains were reburied at Arlington Cemetery. President Franklin D. Roosevelt delivered the oration. ■

in Mississippi. In 1864 he led the only successful foray against Confederate General Nathan Bedford Forest. After the war Karge, assigned to the frontier, gained a reputation for fair dealing with Native Americans. Later at Princeton University he became a professor of European languages and literature.

John Sobieski, a Polish American, was a bugler who was wounded at Gettysburg. He later agreed to serve the United States as a spy in Richmond. He dressed as a Polish nobleman and for three weeks carried out espionage assignments in the Confederate capital.

Immigrants from other European nations from Portugal to Russia served in the Union Army and Navy. In 1862, two Portuguese youths died with a Massachusetts regiment, and others probably served the Union. At least three Ukrainians became officers and others enlisted as soldiers. The only known Romanian American General, George Pomutz of the 15th Iowa Regiment, rolled up a record of bravery at Shiloh, Corinth, Vicksburg, Atlanta, and Savannah.

After serving as a general in the Crimean War, Russian John Turchin arrived here in 1856. He became a colonel in the 19th Illinois Regiment and served bravely in Missouri, Kentucky, and Alabama, where he participated in the capture of Huntsville and Decatur. President Lincoln appointed him a brigadier general. Turchin later wrote the book, *The Battle of Chickamauga*.

No one is sure how many Greek Americans served in the Civil War since only the presence of George Calvorcoresses is known. After landing in the United States, Calvorcoresses graduated from the U.S. Naval Academy at Annapolis. He served at sea from the Mediterranean to Antarctica and from Africa to China.

Calvorcoresses, as commander of the *USS Supply*, captured a Confederate blockade runner. As commander of the *Saratoga*, he earned three citations including one from the Secretary of the Navy.

Carl Schurz had fled Germany. In the United States he was a tireless political campaigner for Abraham Lincoln, who rewarded him with an appointment as a Union general. Schurz did no better or worse than other political generals. His skills were in advancing ideas, not soldiers on a battlefield. Another political general appointed by Lincoln was Swedish American Charles Stolbrand.

Some 10,000 Hispanic Americans fought for the Union. Captain Federico Cavada, a Cuban American engineer, was in charge of the U.S. observation balloons at Antietam, Fredericksburg, and Gettysburg. Captured at Gettysburg and sent to Libby Prison, Caveda later wrote a book about his imprisonment. Another Hispanic American, Lt. Colonel José Chaves, led Union forces that

Admiral David Farragut was of Spanish and French descent.

captured Confederate territories near Albuquerque and Sante Fe.

But the most famous and decorated Hispanic American hero was David Farragut. He commanded the Union fleet that seized New Orleans and helped General Grant capture Vicksburg. His victory at Mobile Bay dispersed the Confederate fleet. To honor Farragut, Congress created the ranks of Vice Admiral and Admiral.

Scandinavian Americans gained a reputation for being dogged soldiers. Between 3,000 and 4,000 Swedish Americans fought in the Civil War. And in July 1865, Eric Bergland became the first Swedish American to be appointed to West Point.

The most famous Norwegian American unit was the 15th Wisconsin Regiment. Of the 900 Scandinavians recruited at Madison, Wisconsin, in 1861 and commanded by Colonel Hans Heg, some had left their homelands less than a year earlier. The 15th fought in 26 battles and engagements in Kentucky, Tennessee, Mississippi, and Alabama. They also pursued Morgan's Raiders, a Confederate guerrilla group. In two days of warfare at Chickamauga, they lost Colonel Heg and many soldiers, but the 15th went on to fight at Chattanooga, to capture Missionary Ridge, and to march triumphantly into Atlanta. With General Sherman, they marched into Savannah and then followed as he cut northward into the Carolinas, a military movement that tore the Confederacy in half. One-third of the 15th Wisconsin died in battle or from wounds.

Norwegian Americans also showed great courage at Gettysburg, where Company H of the 23rd Wisconsin Regiment lost 86 percent of its men. Knute Nelson, born in Norway, was a soldier in the 4th Wisconsin Cavalry and was wounded at Port Hudson. He later studied law, served in the Wisconsin legislature, and in 1882 he became the first Norwegian American elected to Congress and went on to become his state's governor. Elected to the U.S. Senate in 1895,

The Wilson Zouaves, recruited from New York City's lower classes, included many immigrants. They met at Tammany Hall in April 1861, and many brought their own weapons.

Fighting for the Confederacy

Though far fewer in numbers than in the North, immigrants in the South often remained loyal to their states. A thousand Polish Americans and a thousand Jewish Americans were in the Confederate armed forces. Croatian Americans enlisted in the 10th Louisiana Infantry and in four other states' regiments. The "Austrian Guards" was comprised of two Slovenian rifle companies.

Some of the 70,000 German Americans in the South responded to the call to arms. New Orleans had a Jagers German Brigade, Galveston had a German American Battalion, Richmond had two companies, and Georgia a German American artillery company.

One of the Confederacy's most important statemen was Judah Benjamin, a Louisiana Jew born in the West Indies. In Jefferson Davis' cabinet, Benjamin alternated as Attorney General, Secretary of State, and Secretary of War and was called "the brains of the Confederacy." German American Gustav Memminger also served as the Confederacy's Treasury Secretary.

Southern women served as nurses and a few were spies. Disguised as a man, Cuban-born Loretta Valesquez fought at Bull Run and Fort Donelson. She was discharged, reenlisted, fought at Shiloh, and continued to serve until honorably discharged.

On the issue of employing slaves or even free Blacks as soldiers, the Confederacy was trapped by its racial beliefs. "If slaves make good soldiers, then our whole theory of slavery is wrong," said Senator Howell Cobb. But black men were used to build Confederate fortifications. ■

Nelson remained a Senator for four terms until his death in 1923.

Irish American soldiers were sprinkled throughout the regiments of each state. An "Irish Brigade" was composed of four New York Regiments, Pennsylvania's 116th, and the 28th Massachusetts Regiment.

At Antietam, 1,200 Fire Zouaves of the famous "Fighting Irish" 69th New York Regiment under General Thomas Meagher entered the fray, and at parade the next day only 280 could stand. At the Battle of Fredericksburg 1,500 Irish American soldiers marched into battle and only 263 survived.

Irish American Generals such as George Meade, Thomas Meagher, and Grant's Chief of Staff, John Rawlins, helped bring about the final Union victory. Daring Union cavalry officer Philip Sheridan was sometimes compared to Napoleon or Frederick the Great.

General George McClellan was one of many Irish American officers in the Union Army.

Women in the Civil War

White and black women contributed to the war effort. Abolitionist women used the war to agitate for emancipation of the slaves and for racial equality.

At the outset of the war, President Lincoln issued a special appeal to women to aid the Union cause. The response was enthusiastic. Dr. Elizabeth Blackwell organized a Central Relief Committee to train nurses. Until then nursing had been a male occupation. Veronica and Thadia Klimkiewicz, Polish-Lithuanian Sisters of Mercy, cared for both Union wounded and smallpox victims.

Mary Livermore and Jane Hoge became leaders of the Union's Sanitary Commission. The Commission saw that hospitals were staffed with nurses, supplied with medicine, clothing, and food, and given advice on hygiene and sanitation.

Some Northern women served at the battlefront. Clara Barton nursed wounded soldiers as bullets flew around her during the Battle of Antietam. It took Dr. Mary Walker three years to get a Union Army appointment and then she was captured. A few women dressed as men to serve in the Union Army.

Slave women aided the Union cause in many ways. Tens of thousands of runaways who fled to the Union lines volunteered to keep Army camps clean or served as nurses, cooks, and launderers.

Susie King wrote of the African American women who risked their lives behind Confederate lines to save captured Union troops.

> There were hundreds of them who assisted the Union soldiers by hiding them and helping them escape. Many were punished for taking food to the [Confederate] prison stockades.

Slave Mary Bowser and her owner, Elizabeth Van Lew, formed a spy team. When Bowser took a job in Confederate President Jefferson Davis's office, she pretended to be dull. Then she gained access to information for Van Lew, who relayed it to Northern officers.

A slave named Dabney provided General Joseph Hooker with valuable Confederate secrets. Dabney's information came from his wife, a launderer for the Confederate troops. By hanging out her laundry in a special code, she managed to relay information about Confederate plans.

During the war, a brave band of New England schoolteachers of both races came South to teach the former slaves. Among them was Charlotte Forten, who had been born to a wealthy African American family in Philadelphia. She gave ex-slaves some of their earliest lessons in reading, writing, history, and citizens' rights.

Susie King, at 14, also took a job as a teacher of former slaves:

> I have about forty children to teach, besides a number of adults who come to me nights, all of them so eager to learn to read and write... above everything else. ■

No one questioned the Irish American ability or will to fight. What was doubted was their willingness to serve an army that marched against slavery. Just days after Irish Americans died by the hundreds at Gettysburg, New York City's draft riots broke out. Mobs of poor, largely Irish American men attacked defenseless Blacks. After three days of uncontrolled rioting, U.S. troops had to be recalled from Gettysburg to quell the violence in New York.

Many French Canadian Americans born in Canada or France served the Union cause. Among them was General John Buford, who fired the first shot at the Battle of Gettysburg.

Jewish American enlistees numbered more than 6,000 in the Union Army and Navy, and Jewish officers included nine generals, 18 colonels, 40 majors, 25 surgeons, and more than 500 captains and lieutenants. At Bull Run, Max Einstein from Germany commanded a regiment that included about 90 Jewish Americans. In Chicago and Syracuse, Jewish American soldiers formed special companies, but mostly they marched alongside others in state regiments.

Seven Jewish American soldiers earned the Congressional Medal of Honor. Leopold Karpeles arrived from Prague at age 12 in 1838 and settled in Texas. He enlisted in a Massachusetts regiment and in a disorderly retreat during the Battle of the Wilderness, Karpeles saved many others. At the Wilderness, Abraham Cohn, from Berlin, Germany, rallied troops while under heavy fire. Ben Levy enlisted at 16 in the 1st New York Regiment as a drummer. While at sea he saved a Union ship from capture. Leopold Blumenberg had to flee Baltimore because of his antislavery views. Serving in a Union regiment he had helped organize, he was wounded at Antietam. Colonel Edward Solomon commanded the 82nd Illinois Regiment, which had more than 100 Jewish Americans. He fought at Gettysburg and Atlanta, and after the war he became the Governor of the Washington Territory.

However, Jews were not always welcome in Union ranks. Early in the war a Jewish American delegation had to convince President Lincoln that rabbis should serve as chaplains. Six months later, in June 1862, Grant issued Order No. 11, which banned Jewish American peddlers from his camps. Since this order undermined morale and caused widespread protests, Lincoln quickly revoked it.

CHAPTER 5

THE WAR AGAINST SLAVERY

The war to preserve the Union soon turned into a struggle for freedom, and people the world over were inspired. Working men and women in Europe demanded their governments end all trade with the Confederacy. No government dared recognize the Confederacy. In England, where textile mills depended on Southern cotton, workers met and voted to support the Union and its war against slavery.

Some foreign visitors tried to help the Union. In 1864 Polish and Lithuanian sailors deserted Russian ships in New York harbor to enlist in the fight for freedom. The Czarist government tried to extradite the deserters, but American Czechs, Poles, and Lithuanians held huge meetings in New York City that won the deserters the right of asylum and a chance to enlist.

For ethnic minorities the Civil War was a chance to demonstrate their patriotism and courage. For African Americans patriotism and daring became their means of freeing their sisters and brothers.

When graycoated and bluecoated armies first met in battle, slaves saw freedom in their future. Long before President Lincoln signed the Emancipation Proclamation, the enslaved saw Union soldiers as liberators and the war as deliverance.

Lincoln's election in 1860 triggered slave revolts. In Natchez, Mississippi, a slave named Mosely announced "Lincoln would set us free." He plotted an armed rebellion to coincide with the President's inauguration day. A white Texan wrote, "We sleep upon our arms and the whole country is deeply excited."

In the North, free black men found the War Department did not want their help. Lincoln stated that he intended to save the Union and did not intend to interfere with slavery. In 1862 he said, "If I could save the union without freeing any slave, I would do it."

Union generals offered to crush any slave rebellions. Officers returned runaway slaves to their Confederate owners. Confederate officers were allowed to enter Union camps and claim fugitives. Even the Hutchinson Family Singers were barred from entertaining at Union camps because they sang antislavery songs.

But as slaves fled to the Union lines the policy began to change. Why reject slaves who fled the enemy, especially when they offered to help? Why return laborers to an enemy? The sight of Confederate officers retaking and beating their slaves infuriated some Northern soldiers. Irish Americans in the New York Fire Zouaves, General Daniel Sickles reported to Congress, "would go out and rescue the Negro, and in some instances would thrash the masters."

Slave runaways brought pressure for change. In May 1861, U.S. General Ben Butler of Fort Monroe, Virginia, altered Union policy. He declared slaves "contraband of war" and refused to return them to their Confederate masters. The news traveled swiftly. By July, Butler had 900 fugitives as his guests, by Christmas, 3,000.

Generals and officers, facing a steady stream of black refugees, continued to bend Union policy. In February 1862, when General Don Carlos Buell ordered slaves returned, his junior officers refused to return those with military information. In enemy territory some officers found "the slaves were our only friends." Alexander Jekelfabussy, a Hungarian American officer in the 24th Illinois Regiment, resigned rather than return any runaways.

By March, General Ambrose Burnside reported increased numbers of runaways in North Carolina. These former slaves, he said, "find their way to us through the woods and swamp from every side." By August a Confederate officer estimated that a million dollars in slave property fled the South weekly. Florida's Governor was asked to declare martial law in six counties. "Traitors and lawless Negroes," he was told, were waging war against the Confederacy.

Some U.S. soldiers, inspired by the determination of slaves to gain freedom, secretly aided those making their escape. At Camp Jackson, German Americans from Missouri carried into battle a red flag showing a hammer smashing the handcuffs of slavery.

For the enslaved, wartime suddenly opened a new world. Many slaves were able to leave plantations for the first time to work on fortifications. At the front they observed the weaknesses and strengths of whites and watched in amazement as white officers clashed with each other. The enslaved had never seen so much division among those who claimed to be their superiors.

Next, Union rifle and cannon fire began to tear holes in the power of slave masters. Black people shirked their duties, resisted orders, and some openly defied authority. Slave labor had been the Confederacy's biggest asset. Now it became its worst problem, a powder keg needing only a fuse.

At first there were no revolts. Armies on both sides had pledged to suppress slave rebellions. The Confederacy had increased its patrols. African Americans, wrote a black New York editor, "are too well informed and too wise to court destruction at the hands of the combined Northern and Southern armies."

Instead, tens of thousands of fugitives left plantations to crowd into Union camps. They eagerly volunteered for jobs as laborers, launderers, and cooks. Men asked to be spies or soldiers.

The daring actions of slaves put emancipation on the national agenda. In July 1862, Congress ordered Union officers to stop handing slaves over to Confederate owners. Then Congress authorized the Army to enlist African Americans. Emancipation now needed only President Lincoln's signature and pledge.

On January 1, 1863, the President made emancipation U.S. policy. By then former slaves in the U.S. army had clashed with the foe and shown their military ability in Kansas, Georgia, South Carolina, and Louisiana.

The Emancipation Proclamation did not free anyone. It was largely a symbol and a portent of things to come. The Proclamation declared slaves were free in the Confederacy, where the Union could not enforce the Proclamation. It did not liberate slaves in the four border states that remained loyal to the Union or in those areas of the South which the Union Army had occupied. But the stiff, official words of the Proclamation spelled the end of bondage for any slaves who escaped to Union troops. When Union soldiers gained new Confederate territories, the slaves there became free.

The Civil War officially became a war of liberation. Bluecoats now became freedom-fighters who ended centuries of bondage.

African Americans greeted emancipation with joy. "The day dawns — the morning star is bright upon the horizon," wrote

Frederick Douglass. "The hour strikes for us!" wrote a black New Orleans newspaper in French and English. On the Georgia Sea Islands former slaves for the first time sang,

> My country, 'tis of thee
> Sweet land of liberty,
> Of thee I sing!

President Lincoln and many whites had once thought Blacks would not fight. In 1863, faced with a possible manpower shortage, massive Union recruitment of African American soldiers began. A Southern paper laughed at "the idea of their [slaves] doing any serious fighting against white men."

By the summer of 1863 African Americans had proved their valor and fitness in one battle after another. The black men of the 54th Massachusetts Regiment demonstrated daring when they charged heavily fortified Fort Wagner and suffered 42 percent casualties.

The new soldiers, however, had many complaints. Few were sent to the front and most were used for garrison duty and work details. Those at the front were given less military training and older rifles than white soldiers. They had fewer doctors, hospitals, and medical supplies. For these reasons, 37,300 African Americans lost their lives, a much higher casualty rate than white troops suffered.

Former slave Sgt. Prince Rivers (left) receives the flag from his commander, Colonel Thomas W. Higginson.

Black soldiers made up ten percent of the Union Army.

African American sailors aboard the U.S. Mendota. A fourth of U.S. sailors were African Americans.

African Americans also faced unique dangers. The Confederacy announced that captured African Americans and their white officers would be treated as slave rebels and sold or executed. U.S. General Daniel Ullman found this order only turned his African American troops into "daring and desperate fighters."

African American soldiers entered the war as the North and South were running out of reserves. Blacks' battlefield courage won commendations from their field commanders. Then, in August 1863, President Lincoln said, "the emancipation policy and the use of colored troops constitute the heaviest blow dealt the rebellion." Added Lincoln, "Black troops, with silent tongue, and clenched teeth, and a steady eye, and well-poised bayonet" had helped save the United States of America. A year later he wrote that without his African American troops "we would be compelled to abandon the battlefield in three weeks."

Before the war's end, 178,958 African Americans, a tenth of all Union troops, had taken part in 449 engagements and 39 major battles. Another 29,511 served in the U.S. Navy. This meant that every fourth Union sailor was an African American. A total of 22 black servicemen earned the Congressional Medal of Honor.

Many a white youth from Vermont, Iowa, or Europe gained his

The Capture of the Planter

Robert Smalls grew up as a slave in Beaufort, South Carolina, on the sea islands off the coast. As a boy he was sent to Charleston by his master and took waterfront jobs unloading ships, painting hulls, and making sails. As a teenager he became a sailor and before long he could pilot a boat.

When war came, Smalls was forced into the Confederate Navy as a sailor on the *Planter*, a paddle steamer. He soon became the ship's helmsman and worked with the *Planter*'s slave crew.

In the spring of 1862 the *Planter*'s slave crew met to discuss an escape plan that would involve their wives and children. On the evening of May 12, Smalls and the other African Americans waited until the white captain, chief engineer, and mate went ashore for the day. Then they alerted the women.

At 3 a.m. Smalls sailed the *Planter* out to pick up the families. Then, donning his captain's hat and jacket, Smalls piloted the boat into Charleston harbor.

The *Planter* slowly passed a series of Confederate forts, and at each one Smalls gave the proper signal and was waved on. Then he passed the largest, Fort Sumter, gave two long and one short whistles, and called for more steam. At 5:45 a.m. Captain F. J. Nichols of the Union fleet saw a ship approaching with lowered guns and a white flag. Smalls surrendered the *Planter* to the Union fleet. The actions of Smalls and his crew were proof that slaves were able to help the Union. Smalls became captain of the *Planter*, which became part of the Union Navy.

The news about the *Planter* was not lost on white mothers and fathers in the North. If slaves were willing to help win the war, why not let them? The capture of the *Planter* increased demands that Lincoln emancipate slaves and arm them to fight their masters.

Smalls went on to further fame after the war as a South Carolina state legislator and Congressman. "My race needs no special defense," he once said, "for the past history of [black people] in this country proves them to be the equal of any people anywhere. All they need is an equal chance in the battle of life." ■

first officer's commission leading black troops. Foreigners with exotic names became officers of African American units. Colonel Laszlo Zsulavsky, a nephew of Hungarian patriot Louis Kossuth, helped organize the 82nd Regiment, U.S. Colored Troops (USCT). His brothers, Emil and Zigmond, also became officers in the 82nd USCT. From Argentina, Lt. Colonel Edelmiro Mayer offered himself as a man without prejudices who wanted to lead African American soldiers. He was assigned to the 4th USCT. Andrew Warner, a

Swedish American, was given the command of a company of ex-slaves in the 63rd USCT.

The Civil War did more than end slavery and the Confederacy. It disproved racial fantasies that had labeled African Americans as inferior. Colonel Thomas W. Higginson was the first white officer to command ex-slave soldiers. He wrote, "It would have been madness to attempt with the bravest white troops what I have successfully accomplished with black ones."

African American men, women, and children demonstrated wisdom and daring as they disrupted the Confederate war effort. Many courageously aided bluecoats trapped behind the lines or in Confederate jails. "To see a black face was to find a true heart," said a Union soldier. "Sometimes 40 Negroes, male and female, would come to us from one plantation, each one bringing something to give and lay at our feet," reported an imprisoned Union soldier.

To the white South, complained a Confederate officer, slaves were "an omnipresent spy system, pointing out our valuable men to the enemy, revealing our positions and resources, and yet acting so safely and secretly that there is no means to guard against it!" For these reasons, Allan Pinkerton's U.S. Secret Service often relied on black spies. Mississippi slave John Scobel repeatedly carried out spy missions for Pinkerton.

Lincoln enters Richmond in 1865 and is greeted by its black population.

Union Army invasions of the Confederacy relied heavily on assistance from African Americans. Slaves stopped bringing in the crops the Confederate army needed. Instead, they left plantations to search for loved ones. Outlaw bands that united Native Americans, African Americans, and Confederate deserters left the South in turmoil. Some slaves who knew every road, stream, and target guided the Union troops to their goals. The slaves helped to overturn a social system that had kept them in chains.

The Union Army continued to destroy the Confederacy. In late 1864 General William Tecumseh Sherman cut the South in two and shredded its rail lines. A ragged army of liberated men, women, and children followed in Sherman's wake. At first the General said he would not deal with the people who followed his troops. Then he began to find them a reliable source of information and a work force willing to carry his supplies to the front and defend his rear.

That January, General Sherman met with Savannah's African American leaders. The General then issued Order No. 15, which gave abandoned Confederate plantations on the Georgia Sea Islands to the slaves who had worked on the land. Men and women who had owned nothing all their lives now had their own land.

A new South was born out of the wreckage of war. A soldier found his former master among the captured Confederates. "Hi, massa," he said, "bottom rail on top this time!" A former slave owner confronted a bluecoat who had once been her slave. "Why are you fighting against me?" she demanded. He answered, "I ain't fighting you, I'm fighting to be free."

It was an exciting moment for slaves and their liberators. In 1865, African American troops helped capture Charleston, South Carolina, on February 18th; Petersburg, Virginia, and Wilmington, North Carolina, on February 22nd; and took part in the capture of Richmond, the Confederate capital, on April 3rd. When President Lincoln arrived to tour Richmond 40 hours later, a black cavalry unit escorted him through the Confederate capital.

Liberated slaves were awed by the sight of African Americans in U.S. uniforms. When African American troops entered Wilmington, North Carolina, one soldier described "men and women, old and young were running through the streets, shouting and praising God." One black sergeant said he could "do nothing but cry to look at the poor creatures so overjoyed." "The change," said a black private in Virginia, "seems almost miraculous." In Richmond a black soldier rejoiced, "we have been instrumental in liberating some 500 of our sisters and brethren."

In Richmond, Reverend Garland White's troops asked him as their chaplain to speak about liberty. But words failed him and he began to cry. A few hours later Reverend White was again in tears. After 20 years, he was reunited with his enslaved mother. By helping free their people from bondage, African Americans had made a new start in the land of the free.

CHAPTER 6

FREE AT LAST!

1865 was a year that slave Jacob Stroyer never forgot:

> At last came freedom. And what a joy it brought! The stars and stripes float in the air. The sun is just making its appearance from behind the hills, and throwing its beautiful light upon green bush and tree. The mocking birds and jay birds sing this morning more sweetly than before.

That same year a Union officer in the South saw African American families coming together:

> Men are taking their wives and children; families which had been for a long time broken up are united and oh! such happiness. I am glad I'm here.

When Colonel Charles Fox led his black 55th Massachusetts Regiment into Charleston, whites stayed indoors but slaves came out to celebrate. He recalled the moment.

Colonel Fox (center) leading his 55th Regiment into Charleston, South Carolina, in 1865.

> Cheers, blessings, prayers, and songs were heard on every side. Men and women crowded to shake hands with men and officers.... The glory and triumph of this hour may be imagined, but can never be described. It was one of those occasions which happen but once in a lifetime, to be lived over in memory forever.

To some slaves, liberty meant leaving the plantation and walking down the road for the first time as free men and women.

Others danced or sang for joy. Women put on bright, colorful clothing. People began to search for wives, husbands, and loved ones separated during slavery. There were happy reunions and there was deep sadness when loved ones could not be found. But soon it was time to find a job, a place to live, and begin life anew. People sought an education for their children, some land of their own, and a piece of the American dream.

More than the debris of war had to be cleared away. A social debris remained. Emancipation had destroyed the economic system of the South and its way of life, but what would replace it? Many whites could not accept the fact that black people were free. "If they're not my slaves, whose slaves are they?" asked a former master. Some could not understand why their former slaves would no longer submit to beatings.

The Confederate States had been defeated in the Civil War and the question now was how to integrate these states back into the federal Union. Before he was assassinated in 1865, Abraham Lincoln had developed a plan. His goal was to bring the ex-Confederate states back as quickly and as painlessly as possible. However, Lincoln's plan did little to actively protect the rights of the recently freed slaves and it was opposed in Congress by members of Lincoln's own Republican Party, who were often referred to as "Radical Republicans."

When Lincoln was assassinated, Vice President Andrew Johnson became President. Johnson favored Lincoln's moderate plan for the "Reconstruction" of the South, and soon a major conflict developed between the new President and the Radical Republicans in Congress. In the years 1865-1866, during this impasse in Washington, white Southerners turned to their old leaders for guidance.

At first, former slave masters were in charge and they wanted as few changes as possible. As the dominant power in Southern legislatures, they passed "Black Codes" to replace the old Slave Codes. Under the Black Codes, people of color could not vote, run for office, serve on juries, own guns, or purchase city land.

In most Southern states the Black Codes required each ex-slave to have a white employer or face arrest as a "vagrant." Vagrants were then sentenced to jail and rented out to former masters.

In Louisiana, African Americans had to sign yearly contracts in the first ten days of January and promise to work ten hours a day as farm laborers. Their wages were fixed by a white judge or a white employer, and the ex-slaves could be arrested if they quit their jobs.

Black people soon found they had no economic or political power, and only a few earned and saved enough money to buy their own land.

To find out what was going on in the South, President Johnson sent Carl Schurz, the respected German immigrant, to report on Southern conditions and interview former masters and slaves. Black people, whites told him, "belong to the whites at large." Schurz found planters who tried to keep African Americans nearby so they would "have less difficulty in identifying and reclaiming the slaves belonging to them." Blacks were not treated fairly, he found, but as white "passion" and "profit" saw fit.

Former slaves lived without basic rights. Their churches and schools were burned to the ground. Many who had success in farming or business had their property destroyed or were attacked. In Mississippi, U.S. Colonel Samuel Thomas told Schurz:

> Wherever I go — the street, the shop, the house, the hotel, or the steamboat — I hear the people talk in such a way as to indicate that they are yet unable to conceive of the Negro as possessing any rights at all. Men who are honorable in their dealings with their white neighbors will cheat a Negro without feeling a single twinge of their honor. To kill a Negro they do not deem murder ....

Schurz reported his findings to President Johnson. A poor white from Tennessee, Johnson hated slavery because he knew it also held white people down and forced them to compete with unpaid slave labor. But Johnson ignored Schurz's report and many Southerners began to think they had a friend in the White House.

In 1866 whites rioted against African Americans in Memphis and New Orleans, and the President did nothing. When Frederick Douglass led a black delegation to the White House to demand equal protection of the laws, Johnson said equality would trigger "a race war." Blacks, he suggested, should accept white political rule or leave the South. Douglass and the delegation firmly rejected Johnson's advice.

The Honorable Carl Schurz

Throughout his long political career, Carl Schurz was a fervent reformer. Born in 1829, Schurz was a student at the University of Bonn and in 1848 took part in a German revolution that failed. He had to flee to Zurich, and in 1852 he and his wife came to America.

In 1856 the Schurz family moved to Watertown, Wisconsin, where he joined the new Republican Party. In 1860 he traveled 21,000 miles from Pennsylvania to Wisconsin urging German Americans and others to put his friend Abraham Lincoln in the White House.

During the Civil War, Schurz became minister to Spain. In 1862 Lincoln appointed him a major general and he led his troops at Chancellorsville, Gettysburg, and Chattanooga. His report on postwar labor conditions in the Southern states helped shape the national debate over Reconstruction.

In the fall of 1868 Schurz campaigned to make Ulysses Grant president. The next year Schurz was elected to represent Missouri in the U.S. Senate. He soon became disillusioned with Grant when the President allowed civil servants to be chosen for political loyalty rather than by talent. In 1872 he helped form a Liberal Republican Party. It opposed President Grant but lost the election.

In 1876, President Rutherford B. Hayes appointed Schurz Secretary of the Interior, and Schurz became the first German American to serve in a cabinet post. Schurz campaigned for Civil Service reform and advocated a more humane policy toward Native Americans. Schurz finally became President of the National Civil Service Reform League. ■

Old Confederates felt encouraged and they easily regained power in the Southern states. In 1866 the South elected to Congress, 58 former Confederate Congressmen, 9 Confederate Generals, 6 Confederate cabinet members, and the former Confederate Vice President, Alexander Stephens. Northern Congressmen refused to seat their former enemies and demanded new Southern elections. In Mississippi a former slave owner said:

> We showed our hand too soon. We ought to have waited
> until the troops were withdrawn, and our representatives
> admitted to Congress. Then we could have had
> everything our way.

CHAPTER 7

BLACK RECONSTRUCTION

By 1867 it was clear that the Radical Republicans in Congress were taking control of Reconstruction away from President Johnson. In March of that year Congress passed the First Reconstruction Act. This law divided the South into five military districts and authorized the use of 25,000 troops to occupy the South. The Black Codes passed by the white-controlled Southern legislatures were cut down, and a Freedman's Bureau was established to help ex-slaves adjust to their new lives. The law stated that if a Southern state wanted to be readmitted to the Union it had to hold a constitutional convention under rules set by Congress.

These state constitutional conventions were unique. Blacks voted for them but many whites boycotted the elections. In South Carolina, 76 African American convention delegates outnumbered the 48 white delegates. The Louisiana convention had 49 of each race. Alabama had 90 whites and 18 Blacks; Arkansas, 58 whites and 8 Blacks; Florida, 27 whites and 18 Blacks; Georgia, 137 whites and 33 Blacks; Mississippi, 84 whites and 16 Blacks; North Carolina, 107 whites and 13 Blacks; Texas, 81 whites and 9 Blacks; and Virginia, 80 whites and 25 Blacks.

Former slave masters exaggerated the black participation and ridiculed these state conventions as "barbarism overwhelming civilization." But for the first time in government rich white men were outnumbered by poor and middle-class white farm laborers, ministers, city workers, and former slaves.

Many whites said they feared that African Americans would use their power to demand social equality. But black delegates had more important economic, political, and educational aims. Poor delegates, white and black, used these state conventions to introduce the idea of public

Black members of the Louisiana Constitutional Convention of 1868.

school systems to the South. Long denied a chance for education, the poor now saw education as a magic carpet of opportunity for their children.

The new state constitutions extended democratic rights. The right to vote was granted to all men regardless of race or property. An African American delegate proudly told South Carolina's Constitutional Convention:

Black soldiers, businessmen, and tradesmen line up to vote for the first time.

> I believe, my friends, and fellow-citizens, we are not prepared for this suffrage. But we can learn. Give a man tools and let him commence to use them, and in time he will learn a trade. So it is with voting. We may not understand it at the start, but in time we shall learn to do our duty.

The conventions adopted reforms that had reached Northern states during the age of Jackson. Once the poor had been imprisoned for debt and whipped. Now these practices were abolished. The judiciary was made elective and more responsive to the public. Presidential electors who elected the president were no longer appointed by state legislatures but listed on ballots chosen by the voters.

Following the conventions, newly elected state legislatures passed laws providing state services for physically disabled or the mentally ill. Women were given greater rights than before to own property and gain a divorce. Taxes on the poor were lowered and those on the rich raised. Legislatures voted funds to construct or improve public roads, bridges, and government buildings.

Whites and African Americans had united to create the South's first representative governments. A Northern white, Louis F. Post, who was present in South Carolina, praised the joint effort:

> By every truly democratic test, that Negro-made constitution of South Carolina stands shoulder high above the white man's Constitution which it superseded.

The conflict between the President and Congress worsened during these years. Johnson tried to use his veto power to stop Congressional Reconstruction of the South, but by 1867 the Radical Republicans in Congress had enough votes to override his vetoes.

As Commander-in-Chief of the Army, Johnson appointed Generals who would follow his orders and not those of Congress while administrating the five Southern military districts. Johnson also pardoned ex-Confederate leaders and restored their property to them. This often meant that land which had already been sold to former slaves was seized by soldiers and returned to its former owners.

The President and Congress are shown facing each other as their trains are about to collide.

In 1868 the conflict between the President and Congress peaked when the House of Representatives voted to impeach (indict) Johnson for violation of the Tenure of Office Act. The Tenure of Office Act had been passed by Congress in 1867. It held that the President could not remove certain federal officials from office without the approval of the Senate. When Johnson fired his own Secretary of War, Edwin M. Stanton, the House of Representatives impeached the President.

Under the Constitution, a president cannot be removed from office unless found guilty by the Senate of the charges brought forward in the impeachment. President Johnson was tried by the Senate, which, by one vote, decided not to remove him from office.

Between 1865 and 1870, three new amendments were added to the Constitution of the United States. In 1865, the 13th Amendment was ratified by three-quarters of the states then in the Union and became law. The 13th Amendment abolished slavery.

In 1866, the 14th Amendment was proposed by Congress and submitted to the states for approval. The 14th Amendment made slaves citizens of the United States and protected the civil rights of all Americans. Those ex-Confederate states that had not yet been readmitted to the Union were required to approve the 14th Amendment as a condition of readmission. The Amendment finally became part of the Constitution in 1868.

Lastly, in 1868, Congress proposed the 15th Amendment. This amendment declared that states could not deny their citizens the right to vote because of race, color, or condition of previous servitude. The 15th Amendment was ratified by three-quarters of the states in 1870 and became part of the Constitution.

Many changes took place in the South during Congressional Reconstruction. The Freedman's Bureau helped feed, clothe, and educate ex-slaves by building 4,300 schools and hiring 3,300 teachers. Over the next ten years, through its auspices, over a million former slaves were taught to read and write.

In Natchez, Mississippi, a black mayor ruled a town where children of both races played together. Louisiana experimented in integrated education. "The children were simply kind to each other in the school room as in the streets or elsewhere," reported Superintendent Thomas Conway. But most schools remained segregated.

Former slaves eagerly sought an education. "They are crazy to learn," reported a U.S. official. "Parents," wrote another, "will starve themselves, and go without clothes in order to send their children to school." In North Carolina, an official of the Freedman's Bureau described a classroom he visited: "A child six years old, her mother, grandmother, and great grandmother, the latter over 75 years of age...began their alphabet together and each one can read the Bible fluently."

White teacher Laura Towne (left) was one of many women volunteers who worked to educate ex-slave children.

Adults took classes at night after work. "We work all day but we'll come to you in the evening for learning," an African American farmer proudly told his white teacher.

To meet this hunger for education, Northern churches sent thousands of young Christian women teachers to the South. The young women saw themselves as missionaries of education and in five years they helped increase the literacy rate by 500 percent.

Some whites were infuriated at the thought of their former slaves becoming educated. In one Mississippi county 11 schools were burned down, and not one was left standing. In New Orleans the *Tribune* reported, "The record of the teachers of the first colored schools in Louisiana will be one of honor and blood."

During this period, the Ku Klux Klan was formed as a secret organization seeking the return of white supremacy through violence. The Klan's masked riders targeted African Americans who tried to advance themselves through education and the professions, or by starting businesses or owning land. Klansmen burned churches and schools and terrorized successful African Americans. Its nightriders also struck at whites who stood for racial equality or helped ex-slaves climb the ladders of success.

Despite Klan violence, African Americans were elected officials in ten Southern states. Some became local sheriffs, mayors, and aldermen, and others were Secretaries of State, Superintendents of Education, state legislators, Congressmen, and Lieutenant Governors. Black Lt. Governor P.B.S. Pinchback ruled Louisiana for 43 days when the white Governor was removed by impeachment.

As legislators, former slaves worked hard to bring progress to their regions. In Texas, Richard Allen, an ex-slave who became a legislator from Brazoria County, was responsible in 1870 for the bill that became the Texas Veterans Pension Law. As chairman of the legislature's Roads and Bridges Committee, Allen saw to it that roads and bridges connected Lower East Texas to Jefferson and Hillsboro, and Waco and Dallas County to Corsicana. For his home district Allen introduced a bill for the incorporation of the Houston Furniture Company, and he saw that African Americans had their company, the Houston Mutual Aid Society, incorporated.

Allen's efforts had the support of white legislators such as Eduard Degener. Born in Germany, Degener was devoted to the Union and equal justice in Texas. Two of his sons died fighting for the Union. Degener spoke out for racial equality though his life was threatened, and he was once jailed in San Antonio. In 1868 Degener took part in the Convention that wrote Texas' new Constitution. In 1870 he was elected to Congress, and he never relented in his commitment to voting rights for all men regardless of color.

Congress' attempt to reconstruct the South ultimately failed. The federal government did not send enough troops to force white Southerners to obey the laws. Congress also refused to provide land for the black or white poor who were its main supporters. This left these people landless and powerless. Their enemies still held the reins of the South's economy. Using this economic power and violence, they began to regain political power in the South.

Klan violence hammered at the black-white alliances in each Southern state. Black voters were intimidated or slain. Polling booths were either moved on Election Day so people could not find them or guarded by armed Klansmen and other militant whites.

Klan assaults wrecked the Southern justice system. Judges and

Elias Hill Faces The KKK

In 1871, African American Elias Hill of York County, South Carolina, knew he had to fight the Ku Klux Klan despite the cost. At age seven Hill had become paralyzed. As an adult he was unusually small, had underdeveloped limbs, could not walk, and even needed help to eat. Fascinated by his brilliant mind, white children visited Hill after school and taught him to read and write.

After the Civil War, Hill, known for his strength of character and courage, became a Baptist preacher and community leader. He opened a school for African American children. When some whites accused him of stirring his people to revolt, Hill denied it, saying he was only a loyal Republican. "I believe the Republican Party advocates what is nearer the laws of God than any other party, and therefore I feel that it is right." His religion taught him not to hate whites, Hill explained, but experience taught him to distrust them.

In 1871, Klansmen in York County were on a deadly rampage. In nine months they killed 11 people, injured 600, and burned four black schools and churches. Then they rode out to silence Elias Hill.

One midnight in May about six Klansmen burst into Hill's home. They carried him into the yard, dropped him on the ground, and began to threaten and punch him. They warned him to desert the Republican Party and then rode off. Friends came to Hill's rescue.

When a Congressional investigating committee arrived in York, Hill wanted to testify about the Klan. He was wheeled into the hearing room on a cart, was sworn in, and then eloquently detailed how the Ku Klux Klan menaced American freedom and sought to overturn the United States Congress' rule in South Carolina.

Hill's courage inspired others. Witnesses came forth with evidence that led to the first successful federal prosecution of Klansmen. Arrests and convictions spread to other states. Within a year the Ku Klux Klan closed down its operations. By then Hill and some of his followers had left to find a new home in Africa. ■

juries did not punish crimes committed in the name of racial purity. "The juries were made up of Ku Klux," complained Colonel George Kirk in North Carolina, "and it was impossible for any of the loyal people to get justice before the courts."

African American and white Republicans died together. In Tennessee, in 1868, the Klan attacked a Jewish American store owner and his two African American clerks because as Republicans they practiced equality. The Klansmen lynched the owner and one of his clerks.

The Black Senators from Mississippi

Between 1870 and 1901, 22 African Americans from the South served in the U.S. Congress. Two were Senators from Mississippi. Hiram Revels, a minister who became a Senator, was outspoken in his demands for enforcement of the 15th Amendment that insured voting rights for his people.

Mississippi's other African American Senator, Blanche K. Bruce, was the youngest of 11 children born to a Virginia slave. He escaped slavery, attended Oberlin College, and became a teacher. In Mississippi after the war Bruce was a sheriff, and a super-

Senator Hiram Revels and six black Congressmen

intendent of education. In 1875 he was elected to the United States Senate.

Bruce spoke out for desegregation of the Army. He denounced as selfish and unjust federal policies toward Native Americans. He ended his Senate career trying to save the Freedmen's Savings Bank from bankruptcy. The bank held $57 million in life savings for 70,000 ex-slaves who wanted to buy homes, land, and businesses. Bruce could not save the bank, but his determination rescued and returned three-fifths of the deposits to owners. ■

In 1871 the U.S. government finally outlawed the Klan and jailed some of its leaders in South Carolina, but the violence and intimidation continued. African Americans who voted were fired from their jobs. Their wives were refused credit and service in stores and their children were attacked on the way to school. Middle-class and professional Blacks lost good jobs or saw their farms and businesses go up in smoke. "We soon found that freedom could make folks proud," said an ex-slave, "but it couldn't make them rich."

One by one the Reconstruction governments were overthrown. White supremacy returned to Tennessee in 1869, Virginia, North Carolina, and Georgia in 1870, Alabama, Arkansas, and Texas in 1874, and Mississippi the next year. In the presidential race of 1876, a political deal handed Florida, Louisiana, and South Carolina to white rulers. President Hayes pulled out the last U.S. troops from the South in 1877 and white supremacy soon returned to the region.

NATIVE AMERICANS AND UNITED STATES POLICIES

After the Civil War the federal government continued to confine Native Americans on reservations. In the Indian Territory of Oklahoma the Five Civilized Nations, comprising Cherokees, Creeks, Choctaws, Seminoles, and Chickasaws, had been pressured to side with the Confederacy. This, and the fact that battles between Native Americans and settlers took place during the war, became an excuse to crack down on Indian "traitors."

The Creeks were forced to sell half their territory at 30 cents an acre. The Seminoles had to sell land at 15 cents an acre and then to buy smaller plots at 50 cents an acre.

Native peoples tried to make the best of this aggressive policy from Washington and an expanding white frontier. Those Indian nations with slaves granted them liberty and moved toward equality. Six African American Seminoles were immediately elected to the governing Council. Black Seminole families began to build homes, churches, schools, and businesses.

"Born and Reared" Cherokee

In 1879, African Americans who lived among the Cherokees in Oklahoma demanded equal justice in this petition.

The Cherokee nation is our country; there we were born and reared; there are our homes made by the sweat of our brows; there are our wives and children, whom we love as dearly as though we were born with red, instead of black skins. There we intend to live and defend our natural rights, as guaranteed by the treaties and laws of the United States, by every legitimate and lawful means. ■

Diana Fletcher was one of many African Americans who lived among the Kiowas and other Indian nations.

Cherokees and Creeks also quickly granted equality to their African American members. In 1866 the Commissioner of Indian Affairs reported from Oklahoma:

> The freedmen are the most industrious, economical, and in many respects, the more intelligent portion of the population of the Indian Territory. They all desire to remain in that territory upon lands set apart for their own exclusive use.

Though the Choctaws and Chickasaws moved more slowly toward racial equality, by 1907 the Chickasaws alone operated 21 schools for their black members, and some were integrated into Chickasaw society. This placed the Chickasaws far ahead of white schools in the North and South in 1907.

During the 19th century many whites and African Americans joined Native American nations. Some were attracted by the cash awards the federal government made to settle Native American land claims. But mostly these newcomers were drawn to the Native American approach to family life, society, and law.

The Seminole Negro Indian Scouts

Probably the hardest-hitting unit the U.S. Army ever threw into battle in Texas was a group of four to five dozen African Seminoles. These peerless desert trackers and fighters could race their steeds with grace and use their rifles with pinpoint accuracy.

In 11 years and 26 expeditions the scouts kept the peace on the Rio Grande border. They never lost a man or had one seriously wounded in battle. Four earned the Congressional Medal of Honor, three for riding into a group of 25 Comanche rustlers and picking up Lt. John L. Bullis, their commander, and riding out unscathed. Two scouts did die when they were ambushed by the "King" Fisher gang. ■

The Seminole Negro Indian Scouts

Blacks in Native American villages found justice and educational opportunity. O.S. Fox, editor of the *Cherokee Afro-American*, urged his people, "If you have to make a sacrifice, make it and fill that school up. To be anything, the Indian must be educated."

Missionaries arrived to convert Native Americans into good Christians and to supervise their education. Federal officials increasingly relied on missionaries as experts on Indian life. At the same time speculators and criminals arrived to cheat Native Americans. "Indian agents," hired by the government at only $1,000 a year, were known to be selling food meant for Indians to outsiders.

In 1866 the U.S. Army established its "U.S. Indian Scouts" with pay equal to U.S. cavalrymen. Since many Native Americans could run circles around frontier troops, the Army needed people who knew the terrain and understood desert warfare. In addition, small bands of men had rejected reservation life to live as outlaws and prey on innocent settlers and other Indians.

The federal government tried to end Indian resistance through some peaceful programs. Missionaries were encouraged to run Indian schools and churches. In 1868 a U.S. treaty granted a Navajo Reservation 24,000 square miles in Arizona, New Mexico, Colorado, and Utah, and promised to educate every 30 children who entered classes. Another treaty awarded the Dakota Sioux control of the Black Hills region north of the North Platte River. But this treaty was ignored when gold was found on Indian lands and white trespassers rushed in.

General Ely Parker (right) was part of General Ulysses S. Grant's staff. Grant is at the left.

In April 1869, President Grant appointed his trusted Civil War General, Ely Parker, a Tonowanda Seneca, as the first Indian Commissioner of Indian Affairs. Many people hoped this meant a more democratic and humane Indian policy, but Parker only lasted until 1871. That year Congress announced an end to making treaties with various nations. Then Secretary of the Interior Columbus Delano said "it is our duty to coerce" Native Americans into adopting "our habits and customs."

The coercive program ruled government policies for the next half century. Native American nations were to be defeated militarily and then confined to reservations. People were

These Apaches included Jess (right), a fugitive slave who was a scout at Ft. Apache.

stripped of their right of self-determination and representative government. Their cultural heritage was under attack by teachers and missionaries.

Native Americans responded to these actions with armed resistance. Chiefs such as Nana, Geronimo, and Victorio, who led starving Apaches from reservations, fought the U.S. Cavalry.

White citizens also waged war against the Plains Indians' source of supply — the buffalo. Almost four million buffalo were massacred by whites between 1872 and 1874. Buffalo hides that once cost almost $50 flooded the market and the price fell to a $1 each.

The Flathead nation in Montana's Bitter Root Valley faced another kind of war. White officials tried to tax them and seize their land. In 1876 the Missoula *Missoulian* published a Flathead response:

> Yes, my people, the white man wants us to pay him. He comes in his intent, and says we must pay him — pay him for our own — for the things we have from our God and our forefathers; for the things he never owned and never gave us.... No, no; his course is destruction; he spoils what the spirit who gave us this country made beautiful and clean. But that is not enough; he wants us to pay him besides he is enslaving our country. Yes, and our people, besides, that degradation of a tribe who never were his enemies. What is he: Who sent him here?...He comes like a day that has passed, and night enters our future with him.

Colonel Custer was descended from Hessians who arrived during the American Revolution.

Sioux life came under attack when Colonel George Custer, in violation of a treaty, opened Sioux land in South Dakota's Black Hills to gold prospectors in 1875. He personally led in 110 wagons and 1,200 people including scientists, gold seekers, and journalists. With an eye on the next year's presidential race, Custer rode into battle. But he failed to pay proper attention to a Sioux military genius named Crazy Horse. On his yellow pinto, yelling, "Come on Lakotas, it's a good day to die," Crazy Horse prepared for battle.

At the Battle of Little Big Horn on June 25, 1876, Custer and his command of 266 young men died fighting the Sioux and Cheyenne. Among the dead were 32 Irish American troopers. An African American Sioux, Isaiah Dorman, fluent in six Sioux languages, and a scout for Custer, was mortally wounded. Sitting Bull recognized Dorman as an old friend and offered him a drink of water just before he died. It was the centennial year of the Declaration of Independence and the news of Custer's defeat reached Americans on July 5th. There were immediate calls for the Army to conduct a war of extermination.

After Little Big Horn, the U.S. military noose also closed around Chief Crazy Horse. When he sent nine warriors bearing a white flag to General Miles, Army riflemen shot five. Attacked repeatedly in the winter by U.S. cavalry troops, bands of Sioux saw the choice as death in the snow or surrender.

Crazy Horse finally surrendered his 800 ragged men, women, and children. To turn the event into a victory of the spirit, they entered Fort Robinson, Nebraska, singing. Crazy Horse was later slain in jail. "You have hurt me enough," were his last words. He was 35.

The War Department ordered a roundup of those who had left reservations. Resistance was gallant but futile. Peaceful nations such as the Nez Percé threw their troops against Gatling guns, howitzers, and the firepower of a modern industrial nation.

In 1877, Chief Joseph led his people in a desperate effort to reach Canada. The Nez Percé traded peacefully with whites. When they paused 30 miles from the Canada, they were surrounded by General Nelson Miles' 7th Cavalry. "I am tired of fighting," said Chief Joseph to his people, and continued:

Chief Joseph of the Nez Percé only sought peace for his people.

> It is cold and we have no blankets. The little children are freezing to death. My people, some of them, have run away to the hills and have no blankets, no food; no one knows where they are — perhaps freezing to death. I want to have time to look for my children and see how many I can find. Maybe I shall find them among the dead.
>
> Here me, my chiefs, I am tired; my heart is sick and sad. From where the sun now stands, I will fight no more forever.

The Nez Percé were returned at bayonet point to barren land in Oklahoma where they began to die of malaria.

CHAPTER 9

THE MEXICAN AMERICAN LEGACY

The 2,000 mile Texas-Mexican border that stretches from the Gulf of Mexico in the east along the Rio Grande to El Paso, Texas, in the west has not separated Mexicans from their kinfolk in the United States. In the decades following 1848 an ancient Mexican culture rooted in New and Old World traditions met an industrial, aggressive American society. In 1900 half a million Mexican Americans, people whose ancestry included a mixture of Spanish, Indian, and African forebears, lived on land governed by the United States.

Actually, the American settlers from the North were the real newcomers in the Southwest. But they quickly overwhelmed Mexican Americans with their numbers, energy, and economic and political power. By 1900, whites were outnumbered by Chicanos and Indians only in New Mexico. From Texas to California, white Americans controlled most businesses and the government.

The original Mexican Americans became largely underpaid, unskilled laborers, and many became migratory workers. Some took jobs on ranches as cowboys but rarely became owners or foremen.

Yet, more Mexicans, driven by poverty at home, migrated to the southwestern United States hoping for better paying jobs. In the Southwest, economic opportunity was slight but relatives and friends were many.

Texas cattle, sheep, cotton, and vegetables acted as magnets that drew laborers from Mexico. These new arrivals knew little English and were too busy earning a living to challenge the "gringos," or white Americans, at election time.

Only in the New Mexico Territory did Mexican American political power successfully assert itself. Throughout most of the 19th century, Mexican American legislators dominated the territorial government. But they had to contend with governors who were,

Local Bandits Make Good

Mexican American challenges to United States control were not confined to the legal system. In South Texas, Juan Cortina was a rancher who tried to rescue his people from poverty and U.S. control. In Brownsville, Texas, he once routed local militia and Texas Rangers and issued proclamations demanding equal justice before U.S. Army troops chased his band from town.

To the U.S. authorities, Cortina was Public Enemy #1, but to his people he was a champion and "the red robber of the Rio Grande." In 1873 his outlaw career came to a sudden end when he was captured by Mexican troops. However, he was made a commander in the Mexican army.

In New Mexico in the 1880s, Elfego Baca, another armed desperado, became an idol of his people. He appointed himself deputy sheriff, arrested a white cowhand, and then fought off a band of Texans who rode in to recapture the prisoner.

Baca was seized and tried for murder of some whites but a Mexican American jury found him not guilty. Baca tried to prove that the only language "gringos" understood came from the barrels of a gun. ∎

almost without exception, men appointed by the federal government in Washington.

By the 19th century's end, a majority of Mexican Americans and Mexican immigrants in the Southwest, including women, were farm laborers. They were paid less for the same labor performed by whites and were segregated in special sections of towns. Workers contracted to work for an employer and had to trade at the white employer's store. Since the white boss kept the books, laborers found they were always in debt. To aid family income, Mexican American women had to take jobs, usually at far less pay than white women.

Mexican Americans survived by relying on the strengths of their families and their church. In northern New Mexico, southern Colorado, and the lower Rio Grande region of Texas, a vibrant Mexican American culture blossomed. Proud Spanish Catholic parents surrounded by their large families rejoiced in their ancient heritage and enjoyed their music, dancing, and fiestas.

American rule in the Southwest brought a modern educational system. Mexican American families were pleased their children could attend schools, but most resented the emphasis the white teachers placed on European values and learning English.

These Mexican women in colorful costumes appeared in a California magazine.

CHAPTER 10

THE WOMEN'S SUFFRAGE MOVEMENT

American women hoped and believed the Civil War would lead to their liberation. They had been early and leading abolitionists. They had bravely served as nurses for the wounded and on the homefront. During Reconstruction, they became volunteer teachers and missionaries for the former slaves in the South. Colleges began to admit women, so why not polling booths?

Women voting in Cheyenne, Wyoming, for the first time.

But the 14th Amendment which protected the civil rights of African Americans set women back. The Amendment, in granting rights to "male citizens," for the first time had specifically left women out of the Constitution. However, four western lands — Wyoming, Utah, Colorado, and Idaho — became the first places to adopt women's suffrage in the 19th century.

In turbulent frontier Wyoming, in 1869, there were few women and many lawless men. Its officials believed female suffrage would attract women and families. With that kind of increase in their population, they reasoned, law and order would rule in Wyoming.

Esther Morris, the first woman to serve as Justice of the Peace in Wyoming, helped guide it toward women's suffrage. She invited two candidates for the state legislature to dinner and made each promise that, if elected, he would introduce a women's suffrage bill. One of the candidates was elected, became President of the Wyoming Senate, and introduced a suffrage bill that became law.

The men who ruled Utah, Colorado, and Idaho had special rea-

Women delegates to the 1886 Knights of Labor Convention.

sons for accepting women as voters. In 1870, Utah's Mormons adopted women's suffrage to prove that Mormon women were not oppressed. In 1893, Colorado, influenced by the liberal ideas of the Populist Party, which was composed mainly of farmers and laborers, adopted it. In Idaho, in 1896, it was Mormon voters again who carried women's suffrage.

Meanwhile, women in the East struggled hard but unsuccess-

Education Brings Change to Women

American women found new opportunities for education after the Civil War. Vassar College had opened its doors in 1865, Wellesley and Smith in 1875. Harvard began a college for women in 1882 (later called Radcliffe). Mississippi in 1884 started a state college for women, and Louisiana in 1886 began Newcomb College. In 1890 2,500 women held college degrees. By the standards of their day women paid a high price for their college education. It was an age when women were expected to marry, have children, and work at home. They were not supposed to act as smart as men, even if they knew twice as much.

Education, however, offered new choices. Half of women with degrees did not marry and those who did had fewer children than other married women. Most college-educated women of the day chose a career rather than family life. They quietly blazed new trails. ■

fully for the vote. In 1872, Susan B. Anthony was found guilty of voting in Rochester. She angrily confronted the judge:

> ...you have trampled underfoot every vital principle of our government. My natural rights, my civil rights, my political rights, are all alike ignored. Robbed of the fundamental privilege of citizenship, I am degraded from the status of a citizen to that of a subject, and not only myself individually, but all of my sex, are, by your honor's verdict, doomed to political subjugation under this so-called Republican government.

Despite warnings by the judge, Ms. Anthony continued to argue:

> Your denial of my citizen's right to vote is the denial of my right of consent as one of the governed, the denial of my right of representation as one of the taxed, the denial of my right to a trial by a jury of my peers as an offender against law, therefore, the denial of my sacred rights to life, liberty, property, and....

Finally, the judge ordered her to stop talking and told her to pay a $100 fine and the cost of her trial. She refused. Instead, she

The Beginning of Women's Clubs

In 1868 the New York Press Club refused to admit women journalists to a dinner for Charles Dickens. One of those excluded was a famous reporter, Jane Croly. She decided to form a club, *Sorosis*, to forge "a bond of fellowship" and teach women to think for themselves. The club did not seek any male help.

By the next year *Sorosis* had 83 members — including 22 authors, 11 poets, nine teachers, six artists, two doctors, and an historian. The founding of *Sorosis* marks the beginning of women's clubs in the United States.

In 1890, women's clubs from 17 states united in the General Federation of Women's Clubs. Black women, excluded by these clubs, formed their own associations. These began in 1895 with the National Association of Colored Women. Its first president, Mary Church Terrell, played a leading role in civil rights protests for the next half century. ■

urged women to adopt "the old revolutionary maxim, that 'Resistance to tyranny is obedience to God.'"

Opposition to women as voters rested on entrenched male fears. Some men were threatened by women's equal power and advancement. Politicians feared women voters would demand reforms. Businessmen feared that underpaid women would use political power to press for higher salaries. Some people, including many immigrants, felt that granting women the vote might lead to a breakup of families.

The liquor industry vigorously battled any effort to give women the vote. It feared the growth of the Women's Christian Temperance Union (WCTU), which advocated banning the manufacture and sale of alcoholic drinks. Ethnic minorities who opposed efforts to restrict their drinking habits also counted themselves foes of the women's suffrage movement.

Women marching to protest against saloons.

Some conservative women formed antisuffrage clubs. They argued women did not want or need the vote and claimed women were content to work at home for their husbands and families.

The women's suffrage movement attracted more sympathy than support from women of color. For black women, the issue was not the vote but survival. In the South, violence targeted not only the African American men who voted but also their wives and children. Terrorism against families by the Klan made each man's decision to vote a family matter. Black women were doubly oppressed as workers and as women, so gaining the suffrage remained a low priority.

In the Southwest, Chicano women were concerned with ending white violence and making a living wage for their families. To them the vote was a distant and unfamiliar goal.

Neither Native American men nor women had the vote. They spent their time trying to survive on unproductive reservation land. Each week they had to combat governmental onslaughts on their culture and the education of their children that, along with work, consumed their energy.

Native American women and other women of color worked hard to preserve their cultural heritages. In the privacy of their homes they educated their children and resisted outsiders who would destroy their family and history, their present and future.

CHAPTER 11

BUILDING THE TRANSCONTINENTAL RAILROAD

During the Civil War, Congress authorized the construction of rail lines to unite the east and west coasts of the United States. Congress gave more than 155 million acres of land on both sides of the tracks to railroad companies. Businessmen began to hire their construction crews.

The Union Pacific Company built the railroad from Nebraska westward to Utah. The company hired mostly Irish American crews. But among men also wielding pick and shovel were African Americans and others from Mexico, Canada, Scandinavia, Germany, and other European countries.

Building eastward from California, the Central Pacific Company's Charles Crocker began by hiring Irish immigrants. Then Crocker also began to use Chinese American laborers.

An early strike by Chinese railroad laborers.

In three years Crocker brought over 12,000 Chinese immigrants to work on the railroad. "They are equal to the best white men," he said. "They are very trusty, they are intelligent, and they live up to their contracts."

African Americans and many others also were employed on the Central Pacific rail routes but nine of every ten workers who finished the track came from China. They worked from sunrise to sundown for less than the $35 a month paid whites. Then, in June 1867, 2,000 Chinese Americans laboring in the High Sierras struck for shorter hours. "Eight hours a day good for white men, all the same good for Chinamen," said their leader. They won the monthly salary paid to white laborers.

Chinese work crew building the transcontinental.

In the western mountain ranges, the life of rail workers was hard. In crude shacks, workers had to burn lanterns all day and dig chimneys and airshafts. Often they had to reach work through huge snow drifts. Thousands died in blizzards and snowslides. A company official reported, "The snowslides carried away our camps and we lost a good many men in these slides; many of them we did not find until the next season when the snow melted."

Chinese Americans also died at hazardous tasks on mountaintops. High over the Sierras, suspended in tiny wicker baskets, they placed gunpowder in granite cliffs. Then they lit fuses and tried to swing clear of the blasts. They did not always make it.

Contractors paid labor crews according to the number of tracks laid in the shortest time. Some contractors found it to their advantage to pit one ethnic group against another and to fuel the violence with liquor. Finally, Congressmen warned that funds would be cut off if troublemakers did not halt their violence.

On May 10, 1869, the crews from east and west met at Promontory Point, Utah. Tired men rushed to lay the last few feet of track. There was some drinking and celebrating. The president of the Central Pacific took up a sledgehammer, swung it, and missed the last spike. A howl went up. The vice president of the Union Pacific also missed the spike, and the crowd exploded in laughter. A huge celebration followed.

But something was lacking that day at Promontory Point. Not mentioned by any speaker were the Chinese or other Americans of color whose devotion to task had helped unite the country.

In the 1870s U.S. rail construction continued at a frenzy. In California, Chinese Americans built western sections of the Southern Pacific and Northern Pacific and many trunk and branch lines. Their tracks reached Oregon, Utah, Washington, and Nevada, and penetrated the Mojave Desert.

Other immigrants also helped build America's railroads. In 1865, Swedish Americans arrived in Omaha, Nebraska, and took jobs as skilled blacksmiths, machinists, and carpenters at the Union Pacific rail shops.

More foreigners arrived. After a famine in their homeland in 1867 the first wave of Lithuanians arrived. By the spring of 1869 five of the Lithuanians living in Danville, Pennsylvania, had begun to lay railroad track. In about three years Danville's Lithuanian American community grew to 200.

In 1887 Norwegian Americans helped build the Great Northern Railroad from the Dakotas to Montana. Then they established homesteads in the Great Falls region of Montana. Some later worked in the silver mines to the south and others at Sand Coulee's coal mines.

Rail crews had to cut through forests and mountains.

CHAPTER 12

THE CHINESE SETTLE IN

Most of the Chinese Americans who had built the transcontinental railroad lines remained to take factory jobs. In 1870, 105,000 lived in the United States, most of these in California. By 1875 they constituted 75 percent of San Francisco's woolen workers, 90 percent of its cigar-makers, and a majority of its shoe and garment workers. They built salmon canneries in the Pacific Northwest, Canada, and Alaska, and became pioneer developers of California's abalone and shrimp fisheries.

In California, Chinese Americans were one-tenth of the state's population and made up a fourth of its labor force. Their hands turned swamps in the Sacramento-San Joaquin River delta into rich farm lands. Working as sharecroppers or as independent growers, other Chinese Americans became skilled cultivators and harvesters of vineyards, orchards, and ranches. In Oregon, Ah Bing's unique gift to his adopted homeland was the "bing cherry."

All the Chinese did not stay on the west coast. Some Chinese Americans went to the South to lay tracks for the Alabama and Chattanooga and the Houston and Texas Central railroads.

Chinese Americans celebrate the new year.

Increasingly, Chinese Americans faced illegal attacks and discriminatory laws. San Francisco's Board of Supervisors limited Chinatown to a seven by three block area, thus segregating the Chinese American population. Dennis Kearny, an Irish American sailor, organized a "working man's party" around the popular slogan "The Chinese must go!" His followers ended their outdoor meetings by attacking Chinese Americans on the streets of San Francisco.

Conflict grew. Most emigrants from China were males who planned to work hard, save

their wages, and return home. Men outnumbered women by ten to one. Women did not migrate because they feared the mounting racial violence.

Some Chinese were brought here by labor contractors who worked the Chinese as indentured servants, but Congress stopped this practice. No one hired Chinese immigrants at the salaries given whites, so they had no choice but to accept the wages offered. Union leaders then claimed Chinese Americans did not seek high wages or seek to join unions and thus excluded Chinese American members.

In their segregated Chinatowns, Chinese Americans preserved ancient traditions and drew strength from families, their parents, and elderly relatives. They celebrated their historical legacy. Only a barbarian, said the Chinese, would assault one because of his color or land of birth. And barbarians were not worth fighting.

As they faced increased violence, Chinese Americans realized they had to adopt new tactics. By the 1870s Chinese American merchants formed a self-help group, the Six Companies, to provide community protection and meet their economic and social needs. Based on the six regions of China, the Six Companies challenged

Chinese American Theater

In 1875, a writer for *Scribner's Monthly* said about San Francisco's popular Chinese American theater:

The theater is one of the show places of Chinatown. It will seat nearly a thousand people, and has a pit [orchestra], gallery [balcony], and boxes. The men sit on one side of the house, the women on the other. All are smoking; the men, cigars and pipes; the women, cigarettes.

The performance usually begins at seven in the evening, and closes at two in the morning; but on festive occasions it begins at two in the afternoon, and closes at four in the morning. An historical play is usually about six months long, being continued from night to night until the end. ■

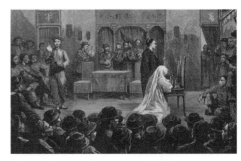

The Chinese theater in California.

discriminatory laws and white terror. In a 1876 letter the Six Companies asked President Grant some pointed questions:

> Are the railroads built by Chinese labor no benefit to the country? Are the manufacturing establishments, largely worked by Chinese, no benefit to this country? Do not the results of the daily toil of a hundred thousand men increase the riches of this country?

A year later the Six Companies reminded their fellow Americans that "self-defense is the common right of all men." By then the group had established patrols in Chinatowns.

Even in Chinatown, whites taunted Chinese Americans. Note the white boys (right) pulling on the hair of a worker.

Chinese Americans also called on officials and friends in China to protest their treatment to the American government. Chinese American newspapers reflected this new attitude which protested against, rather than ignored, white brutality.

But these organized efforts also failed to halt the mounting white hostility. Finally, in 1882, the bigots won a major victory. The United States Congress passed a Chinese Exclusion Act. For the first time an entire people were prohibited from entering the country. Only teachers, merchants, students, and visitors from China were allowed in, and then only temporarily. This law was renewed in 1892, and again in 1902, each time with additional restrictions, and it was not repealed until 1943.

The new law also threatened normal family life. Once Chinese Americans left the United States, they could not return. Men had to decide if they would return to their families in China or live out lonely lives laboring long hours in a distant land.

CHAPTER 13

EARLY NATIONAL UNIONS

The lives of American working people changed dramatically in the decades following the Civil War. Terrence Powderly, an early Irish American labor leader, described some of the changes.

> Articles that were formerly made by hand, were turned out in large quantities by machinery; prices were lowered, and those who worked by hand found themselves competing with something that could withstand hunger and cold and not suffer in the least. The village blacksmith shop was abandoned, the road-side shoe shop was deserted, the tailor left his bench, and all together these mechanics turned away from their country homes and wended their way to the cities wherein the large factories had been erected.

Individual craft workers of the early 19th century knew their bosses well enough to ask for raises, improved labor conditions, and time off. But the millions of factory workers of the late 19th century never met and rarely saw their employers. If they asked for a raise, they might be fired from their jobs.

To improve their pay or conditions, these workers had to unite in unions. They elected union officials who met with bosses to negotiate salaries, hours of labor, and factory conditions.

The first national union in the United States was the National Labor Union (NLU) formed in 1866. In an effort to unify labor, it recruited working people regardless of color, sex, or country of birth. At its first convention, Edward Schlegel of the German Workingmen's Association suggested an independent labor party. His proposal won the approval of the delegates. The NLU was often as interested in politics as it was in solving job problems.

The NLU advocated "justice to women by paying them equal pay for equal work." It started unions among women cigar-makers,

Hardworking New England factory women leave for home.

printers, shoemakers, tailors, and other textile workers. Its leading women's union was the Knights of St. Crispin, which once called a strike that involved several hundred women.

The NLU not only invited women to join but elected them to high offices. It called for state laws that mandated the eight-hour workday for both sexes and equal pay for equal work.

The NLU leaders were equally bold at uniting people across racial lines. At the union's 1869 convention its delegates, 133 whites and 9 Blacks, spoke in favor of a unified labor movement. Isaac Myers, the leading African American union leader of the day, said,

> The white laboring men have nothing to fear from the colored laboring men. We desire to have the highest rate of wages that our labor is worth.

NLU delegates voted to accept African Americans, but also insisted on segregating them in separate locals or clubs. This was an unacceptable compromise for Myers and his followers. Black unionists left with Myers to form their own National Colored Labor Union (NCLU). This union advocated equal rights for women, an income tax, and the unity and equality of workers regardless of color, race, religion, or sex.

Isaac Myers was the first significant black labor leader.

By 1872 the NCLU had become a mere arm of the Republican Party and the union soon disappeared. So, too, did the National Labor Union. It had started by declaring its ranks open to everyone; it had ended by dividing American labor by skin color.

In 1869 Uriah Stephens started a new national union, the Knights of Labor. This new labor organization offered membership

At the 1886 Knights of Labor Convention, black delegate Frank Fanell (left) introduced Terrence Powderly, leader of the Knights.

to "men and women of every craft, creed, and color." It began as a secret society, and was suspicious of employers and interested in reform. It became the first national union to accept both skilled and unskilled laborers as members.

In 1886 the Knights were led by Terrence Powderly, and the membership stood at a high of 700,000. Men and women, Catholics and Protestants, whites and people of color belonged to the union, which boasted 113 women assemblies or locals. In several states, women Knights took part in violent, successful strikes.

In Chicago, the Knights' "Master Workman" was Mrs. George Rodgers. She appeared at one union convention carrying her three-month-old baby, the last of her 13 children.

Mrs. Leonora Barry, another organizer, gave more than 500 lectures for the Knights from Colorado to Alabama. Her investigations of unhealthy and dangerous factory conditions in Illinois led to a strong state inspection law that helped curb child labor in the state.

In the last decades of the 19th century the Knights of Labor lost its momentum. For a brief moment in history it had united labor across racial lines and won some important victories for working men and women.

Oscar Ameringer of the Knights of Labor

Oscar Ameringer, 15 years old and a skilled German carpenter, arrived in Cincinnati in 1886 and found a job in a furniture factory.

> Here everything was done by machine. Our only task was assembling, gluing together, and finishing . . . . Speed came first, quality of workmanship last.

> The work was monotonous, the hours of drudgery ten a day, my wages a dollar a day. Also, Spring was coming on. Birds and blue hills beckoned. And so, when agitators from the Knights of Labor invaded our sweatshop preaching the divine message of less work for more pay, I became theirs.

Ameringer joined a woodworkers' union with a largely German American membership. He later went on to organize African American and white brewery workers in New Orleans. In 1911 he almost won election as mayor of Oklahoma City, and in 1920 in Oklahoma he helped defeat the Ku Klux Klan candidate for governor. Ameringer's life in America also provided the basis for his writing popular satirical works aimed at workers and farmers. ■

C H A P T E R   1 4

MINORITIES IN EARLY STRIKES

Throughout the 19th century, the vast majority of working people were not in unions. In unions or out, they were treated as cogs in an industrial wheel that ground out profits for their employers and for huge corporations. They could be fired or have their wages slashed without notice. If injured by accidents or unhealthy working conditions, employees paid their own bills. They had no vacations, no job security, and no unemployment insurance.

Workers were also victims of an economic system that constantly went through alternating good and bad periods. When the stock market tumbled in 1873 and 5,000 businesses worth over $200 million suddenly failed, breadwinners walked the streets looking for work and for ways to feed families and children. Immigration to America fell by half as this business depression showed the vulnerability of workers in America.

Of all the laborers who had left northern Europe for the United States, Irish Catholics were at first kept at the lowest ends of the job ladder. The United States was basically a Protestant country and Catholicism was often viewed with hostility. In a land that admired farmers and was dedicated to economic and educational advancement, Irish Americans lived in cities, remained poor, and appeared to neglect their education.

Jokes, songs, and newspaper cartoons ridiculed the Irish. Scholar James Ford Rhodes said they had an "heredity bent" for murder. President Rutherford Hayes called them "ignorant and unthinking." But by the strength of their numbers, hard work and determination, Irish Americans began to forge ahead in all areas including politics. The base of political strength in New York City was the Tammany Society which met at Tammany Hall. The Irish in New York controlled the Tammany organization and in 1873

"Honest John" Kelly became "Boss" of Tammany Hall.

In the hard coal fields of northeastern Pennsylvania in the 1870s, Irish American miners had less luck. They tried to survive cave-ins and wage cuts. If they formed a labor union, they would be fired. Instead they turned the Ancient Order of Hibernians, a middle-class Irish association, into their unofficial union.

Franklin Gowan was a wealthy Irish American who employed other Irish Americans to work in his mines and paid them what he chose. At the Pinkerton Detective agency in Chicago, Gowan hired a young Irish immigrant, James McKenna, to act as a spy among the miners. McKenna took the name of McParlan and made friends with the mine workers' leaders. A series of murders and other criminal acts took place soon after "McParlan" went to work for Gowan.

In 1877 the State of Pennsylvania arrested 20 young men for acts of violence and murder. The state's prosecuting attorney was Gowan. McParlan was his main witness. In a trial controlled by Gowan, the 20 men were found guilty and executed.

The *Irish World* called the defendants "intelligent men" who had led "the resistance of the miners to the inhuman reduction of their wages." The *Miners' Journal* asked, "What did they do? Whenever prices of labor did not suit them they organized and proclaimed a strike."

In 1877 thousands of railroad workers, including immigrants and African Americans, launched a strike to halt a sharp cutback in their wages. They had a union but it was very weak.

The work stoppage spread from Martinsburg, West Virginia, east to New York, west to San Francisco, and south to Texas. Trainmen, miners, and other workers together stopped trains. In Baltimore, a strike leader reported widespread public support.

The 1877 nationwide railroad strike united workers of all kinds and was met by violence.

The working people everywhere are with us. They know
what it is to bring up a family on ninety cents a day, to live
on beans and corn meal week in and week out, to run in
debt at the stores until you cannot get trusted any longer,
to see the wife breaking down under privation and
distress, and the children growing up sharp and fierce like
wolves day after day because they don't get enough to eat.

President Rutherford Hayes sent the U.S. Army to break the
strike and in several states troops opened fire on strikers. Hard-
pressed workers, in other parts of the country however, continued
to go on strike. In Marshall, Texas, white railroad workers struck,
then, in neighboring Galveston, black dock laborers struck and won
equal pay with whites. The next day, whites joined their picket lines.

In Louisville, Kentucky, African American sewer workers
struck for $1.50 a day. Work on the city's sewers stopped and in
three days most of Louisville's plants were closed. White copper,
textile, and plow factory laborers then joined the strike.

Strikers tried to ignore racial lines. In St. Louis an African
American unionist asked white strikers if they would stand behind
his levee workers. "We will!" they shouted. In East St. Louis, Illinois,
women supported the male strikers and this action helped bring the
city to a halt.

The unity of strikers across lines of race and sex stirred fear of
revolution among many conservative citizens. A *New York Times*
headline reported Chicago was "in the hands of Communists."

To crush the spreading rail strike, the President recalled 3,000
federal troops from their pursuit of the Nez Percé Indians. Soldiers
were ordered from one struck city to another to restore order and
crush the strike. In Chicago the Army was assisted by local police,
agents armed by employers, and 5,000 deputized lawmen. Some 18
people died when strikers were routed by this combined federal and
local military force. The rail strike of 1877 was finally smashed
through federal intervention. This action sent a message to laboring
Americans and minorities who had united to demand a greater
share of the economic pie. They faced powerful foes and the legal
and military capacity of those who ruled the nation.

NATIVE AMERICANS: THE LAST STAND

By the 1880s the days when Native American hunters roamed the plains were numbered. One of their friends in high office, Carl Schurz, Secretary of the Interior, left office in 1881. Officials who then came to office treated Native Americans as children to be confined on reservations where their culture could be destroyed.

One of the few sympathetic voices left, former slave Senator B. K. Bruce of Mississippi, described the impact of U.S. policy on Native Americans.

> Our Indian policy and administration seem to me to have been inspired and controlled by a stern selfishness, with a few honorable exceptions. Indian treaties have generally been made as the condition and instrument of acquiring the valuable territory occupied by the several Indian nations, and have been changed and revised from time to time as it became desirable that the steadily growing, irrepressible white races should secure more room for their growth and more land for their occupancy; and war, bounties, and beads have been used. . .for the purpose of temporary peace and security for the whites, and as the preliminary to further aggressions upon the red man's lands, with the ultimate aim of his expulsion and extinction from the continent.

In 1881 Helen Hunt Jackson's *A Century of Dishonor* exposed the crimes committed against Native Americans. Jackson said it made little difference where one opened the historical record:

> Every page and every year has its dark stain. The story of one tribe is the story of all, varied only by difference of

time and place; but neither time or place make any difference in the main facts. Colorado is as greedy and unjust in 1880 as was Georgia in 1830, and Ohio in 1795; and the United States breaks its promises now as deftly as then, and with an added ingenuity from long practice ....

Cheating, robbing and breaking promises—these three are clearly things which must cease to be done. One more thing also, and that is the refusal of the protection of the law to the Indian's rights of property, "of life, liberty, and the pursuit of happiness."

The pleas of Bruce and Jackson failed to alter government policies or practices. Neither did the words of Native American leaders who demanded rights written into the U.S. Constitution. In the 1880s federal officials were more influenced by reports from well-intentioned missionaries. White men who had devoted their lives to converting Indians to Christianity and European ways became the government's chosen experts on Indian life.

President Chester Arthur authorized his Secretary of the Interior to ban any Native American customs he thought were "contrary to civilization." Rights to religious worship, dance, and song were ended by the wave of a white hand. Officials in Washington replaced Native American leaders with a stroke of the pen.

It was an age when free enterprise was credited with the nation's huge economic growth. Now demands were made to turn a Native American culture based on cooperation to one based on private ownership. Native Americans were to be instructed in the values of economic competition and land ownership.

Chippewas

In 1887 Congress passed the Allotment Act, which assigned 160-acre tracts of land to each Indian family. But ownership of land by individuals was a European idea. Native Americans did not understand or want it. To them land always meant common use.

The Allotment Act was a disaster. The land it gave to Indians fell mostly into the hands of white speculators. By World War I, Native Americans had lost two-thirds of all their land holdings. The

71

Sarah Winnemucca, born in 1844 in Utah, became a leader of the Paiutes and in 1883 wrote a book, Life Among the Paiutes.

Five Civilized Nations, with 19,500,000 acres in 1887, ended up with a little more than 1,500,000 acres a few decades later. In 1948, the Hoover Commission admitted the Allotment Act "proved to be chiefly a way of getting Indian land into non-Indian ownership."

Native Americans were also subject to an unending assault on their culture. Said T. J. Morgan, Commissioner of Indian Affairs:

> We ask them to recognize that we are the better race; that our God is the true God; that our civilization is the better; that our manners and customs are superior....

The missionaries recommended that government control of Indians focus on their young. Officials removed children from their homes so they could be educated apart from their parents. Some were sent to boarding schools for as long as ten years and forbidden to speak their native languages. During school vacations they were kept from visiting their families and often were sent to work as servants for white families. Native American parents who objected to these practices might find their reservation rations cut.

Federal Indian agents became rich men through graft and theft. Many withheld government blankets, food, and supplies from Indians, sold them, and kept the cash. On one reservation, an agent used food money to finance his mining enterprises. When he was investigated, he sold his mine to the leading investigator, who then bribed the son of the Federal Commissioner of Indian Affairs. Native Americans came to believe that corruption was part of the white way of life. In 1887, at the Powder River Council, Sitting Bull offered his evaluation of white society to Native leaders:

In 1880 at the Carlisle, Pennsylvania, "Indian school" these Native American boys from Nebraska were taught to accept "white civilization."

Home Life Among the Apaches

John Bourke, born to Irish immigrants in Philadelphia, did not see Native Americans the way other whites did. After he graduated from West Point in 1869, he served in the 3rd U.S. Cavalry and spent 14 years in the Southwest. After careful study of Indian life, in 1884 he began to write five books and ten ethnological papers. His *On the Border with Crook* described Apache home life:

Apache leader Geronimo and his wife in 1907.

> Around his own camp-fire the Apache is talkative, witty, fond of telling stories, and indulging in much harmless raillery. He is kind to children, and I have yet to see that first Indian child struck for any cause by either parent or relative. The children are well provided with games of different kinds, and the buckskin doll-babies for the little girls are often very artistic in makeup. The boys have fiddles, flutes, and many sorts of diversion, but at a very early age are given bows and arrows, and amuse them-selves as best they can with hunting.

> They have sham-fights, wrestling matches, foot-races, games of shinny and "muskha," the last really a series of lance-throws along the ground, teaching the youngster steadiness of aim and keeping every muscle fully exercised. They learn at a very early age the names and attributes of all the animals and plants around them. ■

The love of possession is a disease with them. These people make many rules that the rich may break but the poor may not.

In the face of greed and hostility, Native Americans survived through the strong bonds of family and a devotion to traditions. Men and women comforted each other and their children. All drew strength from ancient religions that emphasized the oneness of people and their vital connection to the land.

WOMEN OF THE OLD WEST

The American frontier was the line where European settlements met the wilderness lands inhabited by Native Americans. The frontier was always a moving line, pushed westward from the days of the earliest European landings along the Atlantic coast. In the final decades of the 19th century, railroads penetrated the frontier and settlers filled in the last open spaces. The frontier passed into legend.

Millions of citizens and foreigners were lured to the frontier by the promise of cheap land. For a registration fee of $26 to $34, the federal government granted each head of family 160 acres of land. After five years as a resident, he or she owned the land.

By the time pioneer wagon caravans arrived in the West, some of the best land had already been given away. Congress handed rail companies 180 million acres to build western railroads. Most of this acreage was resold to eager pioneers at a huge profit. At $1.25 an acre, speculators bought more than another half a million acres of good land and this property was resold at a high profit.

Families headed westward each April from such Missouri River towns as Independence, St. Joseph, or Council Bluffs. They hoped to make the trip in six to eight months, but sometimes it took longer. The pioneers' wooden wagons had no springs and were covered by a canvas. The sun sometimes heated the interior to 110 degrees by noon.

Accidents and illness were common. Children fell out of wagons, got lost, or came down with illnesses. More than a few children and adults died and were buried along frontier trails.

Women who began the trip pregnant gave birth in primitive conditions. Some died during childbirth or from diseases. Women whose husbands died on the trip were expected to bury them and then carry on. They had to keep going, and they had to feed and

Annie Oakley, born in 1860, starred in Buffalo Bill's Wild West show for 17 years. She was famous for her accuracy with a rifle.

clothe the children. At their destination, they had to stake the family claim. That meant they had to file a claim for land with a government office. To support their families, some women began businesses, ran boarding homes, or learned new frontier skills.

A woman who may have never wanted to leave home would start out in April with her husband and three children. By December she might be living as a widow with a baby and two children on a prairie far from home and relatives. Only strong faith and gritty determination carried such women across the continent.

There was at least one reward for women who endured frontier conditions. The four states that adopted women's suffrage in the 19th century were in the West, and the first seven states to adopt

Calamity Jane served as a scout for General Crook in South Dakota.

Black Women in the Old West

The African American women who headed West were a minority within a minority. Though few in numbers, some had the pluck, determination, and will to succeed as entrepreneurs.

In 1869, Elvira Conley, a tall ex-slave, ran a laundry service in lawless Marshall, Kansas, and two of her best customers were Buffalo Bill and Wild Bill Hickok. In 1874, Virginia City, Nevada, had four hairdressing businesses on C Street run by African American women. The next year, widow Sarah Miner built her husband's hauling enterprise into a $6,000 business, lost it in a fire, and rebuilt it the following year.

Pioneer African American women were an elite breed. Their 74 percent literacy rate was far higher than that of white women, and their 50 percent school attendance rate was equal to that of white girls. They were five times as likely to be employed as white women, twice as likely to be employed as Asian immigrant women or Native American women. Some reached the West as teachers, others as domestic workers, and still others as brides for miners.

African American miners in Arizona met incoming stage coaches and trains hoping to find a black marriage partner. The miners then initiated a brisk business in mail order brides from the East.

Black women, like their white counterparts, brought culture, education, and refinement to frontier communities. They built schools, churches, and community centers. They organized to take care of orphans and the elderly, and collected money for the poor.

They also achieved a level of equality with men that was the envy of their sisters who remained in the East. They managed to overcome obstacles as they reached for success and their American dream. ■

This poster helped bring thousands of African Americans to Kansas seeking homesteads.

Black migrants left the south for Kansas, walking up the Chisholm Trail in 1879.

women's suffrage in the 20th century were also in the West.

In 1879 about 5,000 African Americans left states such as Texas, Louisiana, and Mississippi for the plains of Kansas. With a religious fervor, they sought a new life of freedom for their families.

Many were widows and children fleeing a Klan-type terrorism that had killed their men. "We could do nothing to protect the virtue of our wives and daughters," said a Mississippian. "A poor woman might as well be killed and done with it," said another woman.

These African Americans said they were part of an exodus like the one Moses led out of Egypt, and so they called themselves "the Exodusters." They talked of reaching Canaan in Kansas where their children would be safe and get an education.

Many of these Exodusters lacked the cash for horses or wagons. Some walked to Kansas, dragging or carrying a few belongings. Some had saved enough money to pay the fare of the paddle-wheeled boats that churned up the Mississippi.

Mr. and Mrs. Henry Carter walked from Tennessee to Kansas. She carried the bedclothes, and he toted the tools. In a year they had jobs with sheep ranchers, bought and cleared 40 acres, built a 16-foot stone home, and owned a horse and two cows.

The Exodusters survived many dangers. Organizers for the exodus were driven from towns or beaten. Whites in Mississippi had closed the river to African Americans and threatened to sink boats that carried them. In terse military terms, U.S. General Thomas Conway reported events to President Rutherford Hayes:

Every river landing is blockaded by
white enemies of the colored exodus;
some of whom are mounted and armed,
as if we are at war.

But neither Southern violence, Northern resentment, nor a congressional investigation stopped the exodus. The sudden arrival of thousands of poor people strained relief facilities in Kansas towns. Black families and white families helped the newcomers. Some arrivals then headed into the countryside to stake out homesteads on the plains of Kansas and neighboring Nebraska.

CHAPTER 17

IMMIGRANTS HEAD WESTWARD

For tens of thousands of landless peasants in Europe, the federal government's homestead policy to settle the frontier was an irresistible magnet. To be granted his or her 160 acres, the head of an immigrant family only had to promise to become a citizen, to live on the land for five years, and to pay a small registration fee. In vast caravans of wagons, on trains or on horseback, foreigners and citizens poured into the western territories.

By 1870, half of the men 21 and over living in Arizona, California, Nevada, Utah, and Idaho had been born abroad. Some were from lands as distant as Russia and China; others were from neighboring Mexico and Canada. Thousands more were ex-slaves.

The frontier receded before the rush of these pioneers. By 1880, Kansas had 850,000 people and Nebraska had 450,000. Between 1880 and 1885 the Dakota Territory, comprising present-day North and South Dakota and much of Montana and Wyoming, had increased from 55,000 people to 550,000. By 1890 North and South Dakota, Washington, Montana, Wyoming, and Idaho had been admitted as states; Montana had 132,000 settlers. On the streets of frontier towns one could hear accents from Rome, Stockholm, or Moscow.

A Czech Builds a Prairie Sod house

In 1891 Czech immigrant Joseph Pecinovsky wrote in *The Almanac Amerikan* of how his family built their first home.

With hoes we raked a patch of ground to plant potatoes. Our house was a very simple affair. We dug a hole in the ground, lining it with sod. Then we threw a top over it, overlaid that with brushwood and thatch and our dwelling was complete. ∎

Scandinavian immigrants sought out new homes on the frontier. By 1868 a Norwegian newspaper, *Nordiske Folksblad*, was published in Rochester, Minnesota. That same year Swedish immigrants arrived in Chicago seeking a site for a Swedish Lutheran community and eventually settled in Kansas' Smokey River valley.

Swedish immigrant Knute Steernerson led pioneers beyond the last white settlements to the Minnesota River valley. Soon their farms stretched for 50 miles, with Montevideo at the center.

To encourage settlement, many western states established immigration boards and hired foreigners to locate community sites and to bring in settlers. In 1869 the first Swedish American newspaper was published; its aim was to attract more families from Sweden to the American West.

Swedish Americans poured into Nebraska and then Minnesota. By 1870 a Swedish American, Hans Mattson, had been elected as Minnesota's Secretary of State. He was the first Scandinavian immigrant to be elected to high public office.

Scandinavian Americans also pushed into the triangle of land between the upper Mississippi River and the Missouri River. By 1870, Iowa had 3,000 Danish Americans. Many started as railroad workers or farmhands, but managed to save enough money to begin their own dairy farms. Some pooled their cash to start cooperative creameries in which the profits were shared. Between 1872 and 1892 Danish Americans established four newspapers in the West.

By the 1870s, Midwestern politicians carefully courted Scandinavian American voters. Republicans in Minnesota began to distribute campaign literature in Swedish. In 1880 a Swedish American, Thomas Bayard, was appointed Secretary of State in Democratic President Grover Cleveland's cabinet. By 1890, the newcomers held major state offices in Minnesota.

Scandinavian immigrants entered the Dakota Territory in force in the 1870s. When enough people arrived they began Augustana College in South Dakota to train their theologians. In 1879 Sioux Falls had its first Norwegian American paper, and in eastern Dakota it was said that one could more quickly find a person who spoke Swedish than one who spoke English.

By 1880 some 20,000 Norwegian Americans lived in the Dakota Territory. Nine years later one of them, lumber and mining baron

Anton Holter, was elected to the state legislature. Some families later left to build homes and farms in the Pacific Northwest.

In 1882, Norwegian and Danish migration reached a peak. Between 1879 and 1893 more than a quarter million Norwegians poured into the United States. A "New Norway" stretched from Lake Michigan west to the Dakotas and to the Missouri River. In the 1880s, Swedish migration peaked when it reached more than 400,000 people.

Within a decade 400 Minnesota towns bore Swedish names. In Montana's Crazy Mountains and Flathead Mountains, American Swedes and Norwegians settled in pioneer communities founded earlier by immigrants from Scandinavia.

The newcomers sometimes came together for cultural or political purposes. For example, the United Scandinavian Singers of America recruited American Danes, Norwegians, and Swedes devoted to the folk music of their homelands. In the Dakotas, Scandinavian Americans united to oppose a law requiring the schools to teach in English. In Illinois and Wisconsin, they joined other Europeans also to force the repeal of laws that required all school instruction be in English.

The Goldwater Brothers of the West

During the Civil War, Jewish peddlers Joseph and Michael Goldwater came to Arizona and opened "Goldwater and Brother" stores in Phoenix and in Prescott. They began a freighting concern to service the needs of the U.S. Army. In 1866, when Michael was slain by a desperado, Joseph carried on the family business. One of their descendants, Barry Goldwater, became a Senator and the 1964 Republican candidate for President of the United States.

The Goldwaters were among many Jewish American merchants who delivered dry goods to a frontier craving eastern finery. In 1861 traveler Henry A. Tilley wrote of these early salesmen:

> The Jews brought their old predilections into the new world, and are quite in their element among piles of ready made clothing and boxes of cigars. But to their credit let it be said that they have also brought with them their industry, perseverance, and love of order which make them good citizens. ■

THE LONG CATTLE DRIVES

After the Civil War, five million cattle roamed free and wild in Texas. Western railroads suddenly made these maverick steers valuable. If they could be brought to rail junctions, steers could then be shipped to Chicago or Kansas City where they were sold for $30 to $40 a head. After being slaughtered, the meat was transported to expanding, hungry city populations.

The first path to the rail junctions in Kansas was blazed by Jesse Chisholm, a frontier explorer of Cherokee and European blood. In 1866, he began to run wagons loaded with buffalo hides from Oklahoma to Kansas. Chisholm's wagon wheels cut deep ruts in the prairie soil. Cowboys later named it the Chisholm Trail.

At the end of the Chisholm Trail was Abilene, Kansas, with its Kansas Pacific Railroad line to Chicago. By 1867 the town became a principal destination for cattle drives. As the first big cowtown it received one and a half million head of cattle per year by 1872.

On a large cattle drive, a trail crew coaxed and prodded an average of 2,500 or more head of cattle. Trained hands stood ready to load 40 cattle-cars every two hours. Long trains of cattle-cars then sped the animals to Chicago slaughterhouses.

Cowboy skills were first developed by Mexican Americans and then learned by white and black cowhands.

At the heart of these "long drives" to Kansas over the next three decades were 35,000 cowhands. The average trail crew of 11 was a uniquely American mixture that usually included two or three African Americans and one or two Mexican Americans or Native Americans. George Saunders, president of the Old Time Drivers Association, recalled that between 1868 and 1895 "about one-third of the trail crews were Negroes and Mexicans." For $30 a month and grub, cowhands signed up for a perilous journey of two to three months. The men had to outlast storms and stampedes, droughts and landslides, and dangers from man and beast.

After 1873, when Joseph Glidden invented barbed wire, the western landscape changed forever. The U.S. had been fenced in.

Owners of sturdy longhorns, though a minority, ruled the cattle country. Not lawmen with badges but live-stock associations formed by cattle owners decided the thorny questions of who owned what land and which cattle. Native Americans had no voice in the change. By 1880, much of the plains from Canada to the Rio Grande and from the Mississippi to the Rockies was cattle country.

Bill Pickett (middle row, third from right) was the featured act of the 101 Ranch Rodeo. He was assisted by Will Rogers (two to the left of Pickett), Tom Mix (two to the left of Rogers), and an Italian American who rode in from Canada.

Against this background, American cowhands tried to preserve their self-reliance and individualism. Still these were men whose lives depended on cooperation. In 1883 Mexican American Juan Gomez led several hundred cowpunchers in the Texas panhandle in history's first strike by cowhands.

Some cowpunchers left a permanent imprint on the West. The three Miller brothers rounded up the best cowboy talent they could find to work their huge, sprawling 101 Ranch in Oklahoma. Their star cowhand was Bill Pickett, who had been born in 1870, the second of 13 children of African American and Cherokee parents. After completing the fifth grade, Pickett left school for the range where he developed roping and riding skills, and a unique technique for wrestling steers called "bulldogging." The 5-foot 7-inch Pickett could leap from his horse onto the back of a 500-pound steer, grab a horn in each hand, and wrestle the steer to the ground.

Lawlessness was commonplace on the frontier. The first man placed in Abilene's new stone jail was a black cowhand, a cook for a Texas trail crew. Furious over his arrest, his trail crew rode into town, pulled the bars from his cell window, rescued the cook, shot up the town, and rode off. No one rode after them.

One of Dodge City's cattle rustlers was Ben Hodges, of African American, Native American, and Mexican American ancestry. Some

Black cowboy Nat Love headed west at 16 and became famous as "Deadwood Dick" when he won roping and shooting contests in 1876 in Deadwood City, Dakota Territory. He wrote a book about his exciting adventures.

"Stagecoach Mary" Fields

Mary Fields was born in a Tennessee slave cabin when Andrew Jackson was President. Six feet tall, 200 pounds, she became a legend soon after she arrived in Cascade, Montana, in 1884.

Her first job was hauling freight for St. Peter's Catholic Mission. Her wagon once overturned on the prairie and she spent the night fighting off wolves with her revolver and rifle. When she and a white cowman had a shoot-out, she lost her job.

Fields went into town where she ran a laundry. When a man picked up his laundry and refused to pay, she trotted after him, tapped him on the shoulder and laid him out with a right cross to the jaw.

In 1895, Fields, in her sixties, landed a job delivering the U.S. mail and driving a stagecoach. She became "Stagecoach Mary." Stories about this legendary figure were related by actor Gary Cooper. At age ten, in Cascade, he was one of her many admirers. ■

said he had the fastest tongue in the West. He talked the manager of the local bank into lending him money and the head of the railroad into giving him free passes. Hodges was brought to trial several times but never sent to prison. Then he applied for a job as state livestock inspector, but those who knew him went to the Governor to make sure the fox was not put in charge of the henhouse. Hodges died in 1929. When they carried his body up to the Maple Grove cemetery, someone asked a pallbearer why Hodges was to be buried among the best citizens of Dodge. He answered, "We want him where they can still keep an eye on him."

African Americans rode with Billy the Kid and in the forces sent against him. Native Americans and African Americans were among the deputy sheriffs dispatched by Judge Isaac Parker to bring peace to the troubled Oklahoma Indian Territory. African American deputy Bass Reeves, the Territory's best known lawman, served Parker for 37 years. Only one man, Hullubee Smith, ever slipped past the nets he cast.

African American Barney Ford owned large hotels in Denver and Cheyenne.

Reeves said he relied on his disguises and detective skills and always avoided shoot-outs. However, he did admit to slaying 14 men, each of whom (he said) drew on him first. Reeves never was wounded, though a button was once shot off his shirt, his belt was shot in two, and his hat brim was shot off.

THE FRONTIER U.S. ARMY

From the Canadian border to the Rio Grande and from the Mississippi River to the Rockies, the U.S. Cavalry was often the only evidence of U.S. law. Many of the recruits, perhaps half, were immigrants from Ireland, England, and Germany, with some from Canada, Scotland, Croatia, and Switzerland. The cavalry ranks were filled with such names as Smith, Jones, Taylor, Frascola, Kurz, Sobl, Roque, and Mazzanovich.

The post-war Army had lost its Civil War glory. Citizens began to rank soldiers with dogs and vermin. In Texas, troopers met scorn at the hands of Confederate veterans. Doors were shut in their faces. Parents hurried daughters and children inside when soldiers appeared, and businessmen refused soldiers service.

But for African Americans the military offered dignified, satisfying "man's work." Denied decent civilian jobs after the Civil War, their morale and accomplishments were highly praised by their white officers in the Army.

Tenth Cavalryman, sketched by artist Frederic Remington.

Four black regiments served in the West, the 24th and 25th Infantry and 9th and 10th Cavalry. Called "U.S. Colored Troops," they rolled up an impressive record of valor on the frontier. "Buffalo Soldiers," as they were named by Native Americans, enforced law and order and guarded towns, stagecoaches, and trains.

Headquarters supplied white regiments with a silk-embroidered flag but the regimental banner of the black 10th Cavalry was homemade, faded, and worn.

Animosity toward the U.S. Army in Texas sometimes united the soldiers of both races. In 1881, after an African American private was slain by a gambler and a white private was killed by another civilian in San

Native Americans called African American troops "Buffalo Soldiers."

Oklahoma

By the 1880s only the Oklahoma Indian Territory remained untouched by white settlement. It was home for 22 Indian nations that had been settled by the government on largely barren land. Federal officials gave their solemn assurance that Oklahoma's reservations would belong forever to Native Americans, and the U.S. Army protected Oklahoma from intruders.

However, as the frontier disappeared, officials came under a relentless pressure to open Native American lands. In 1889 Congress announced that 1,920,000 acres of Oklahoma would be open to homesteaders. A month before the designated day of the rush to claim the newly opened lands, roads to the starting point were jammed with citizens of every background, color, and tongue, including 10,000 African Americans.

On April 22, 1889, 100,000 people amassed at noon for the land rush. Men, women, and children waited impatiently on horses, bicycles, buggies, wheelbarrows, and on foot. At a signal they raced into the territory to claim land.

Within a few hours entire districts were settled. By nightfall Oklahoma City had 10,000 citizens living in tents and the city of Guthrie had almost 15,000 residents. In both places businesses opened the next morning. Within weeks towns had picked government officials. By 1890 western Oklahoma was a United States Territory.

Edwin P. McCabe

Inroads were made on other Indian lands in Oklahoma. In September 1891, 900,000 acres owned by the Potawatomi and Sauk and Fox were opened to outside settlers. In April 1892, the 3,000,000 acres of the Cheyenne-Arapaho reservation were opened, and in September 1893, another 100,000 eager pioneers lined up and charged into another 6,000,000 acres.

Edwin P. McCabe founded the town of Langston, Oklahoma, edited its newspaper, and began to work on his dream. His agents traveled into the South armed with railroad tickets and brochures offering Oklahoma as a black homeland. Politically ambitious, McCabe wanted to place himself in the Governor's chair of Oklahoma.

Realizing it was futile to try to win African American political power in the Oklahoma Territory for his people, McCabe concentrated on aiding arriving families. From 1890 to 1910, 30 self-governing all-black towns were formed in Oklahoma.

When McCabe organized his people for the September 1891 land rush for more Oklahoma land, he was fired on by white riflemen. These whites were finally driven away when friends of McCabe arrived with their own Winchester rifles.

African Americans next concentrated their energies on keeping Oklahoma from becoming another segregated Southern state. They formed an Equal Rights Association, a Suffrage League, a Negro Protective League, and many other local groups. In Muskogee in December 1906, 300 black citizens protested the election of an all-white Oklahoma Constitutional Convention.

In 1906 the Oklahoma Territory boasted 500,000 citizens, and more than 100,000 were African Americans. In November 1907, Oklahoma became a state with a full set of segregation laws that kept people of color from sitting next to whites in schools, streetcars, or public buildings. Oklahoma even became the first state to segregate telephone booths. ■

Town Council of Boley, Oklahoma

Major Charles Young was one of three black men to graduate from West Point in the 19th century.

Angelo, Texas, cavalrymen of both races posted a warning:

> We, the soldiers of the United States Army, do hereby warn cowboys, etc., of San Angelo and vicinity, to recognize our rights of way as just and peaceable men. If we do not receive justice and fair play, which we must have, someone will suffer; if not the guilty, the innocent. It has gone too far; justice or death.

> U.S. Soldiers, one and all.

Some 18 African Americans earned the Congressional Medal of Honor on the frontier. The first was Emmanuel Stance who, in five encounters with Plains Indians, won unstinting praise from his commander. The daring of others who earned the Medal was buried in terse military phrases such as "bravery in action," "gallantry in hand-to-hand combat," and "saved the lives of his comrades."

It was ironic that these brave African Americans played a role in the final defeat of Native American nations. But they had taken a job in which the orders came from Washington and Generals who had decided that "the only good Indian is a dead Indian."

The Buffalo Soldiers won the admiration of every friend and foe they faced. General John J. "Black Jack" Pershing was proud to have earned his nickname leading the 10th Cavalry in Montana and on the Mexican border. His cavalrymen, he said, "had always added glory to the military history of America."

Before he commanded American troops in World War I, General John J. Pershing earned the nickname "Black Jack" leading the 10th Calvary regiment in Montana.

The Buffalo Soldiers served under white officers because there were few, if any, black officers. Although 20 African Americans were admitted to West Point in the 19th century, they had to run a hate-filled gauntlet and only three finally graduated. One African American cadet was found tied to his bed, his hair cut, and his ears slashed. He was blamed for causing his own injuries and was expelled.

Finally, in 1877, Henry Flipper, son of Georgia slaves, graduated 50th in a class of 76. He was later court-martialed and forced out of the military on trumped-up charges that were finally reversed in 1989. In 1887 John Alexander graduated, served for seven years as an officer of the 9th Cavalry, and died on duty. Charles Young graduated from West Point in 1889 and was assigned to the 10th Cavalry. He served bravely in the Spanish American War and with General Pershing's troops in Texas.

OVERCOMING ODDS

For African Americans the decades that ended the 19th century were a battle against adverse odds. Ninety percent of African American families lived and worked in the South, 80 percent in rural areas. By 1900 a good percentage of all black farmers were landowners and held property amounting to a billion dollars. But the vast majority of black people were poor share-croppers, and those who dared challenge their bosses or landlords faced a legal system of white sheriffs, legislators, judges, and jailers.

Despite discrimination, an educated African American middle class began to grow in America's cities. By 1900 this middle class included more than 15,000 preachers, 21,000 teachers, 1,700 doctors, 210 dentists, 728 lawyers, as well as actors, poets, sculptors, photographers, architects, draftsmen, journalists, and inventors. Black-owned businesses included four banks, 64 drug stores, and many small enterprises that served their communities. Charles Graves, president of the company that owned mines in Illinois and Montana, became the first African American millionaire.

In 1891, white reformer Samuel Barrows traveled 3,500 miles in the South to survey black education and progress. African Americans, he found, had an interest in education that in some places "amounts to an absolute thirst." At Tuskegee College, launched a decade earlier by ex-slave Booker T. Washington with only 30 pupils, Barrows found 450 students and 31 teachers. Of its 14 school buildings, eight had been erected by the students. Barrows also found that African American communities had developed a network of self-help organizations to "care for their own poor."

Sharecroppers, adults and children, had to work long hours in the hot sun.

Black adults were denied access to most white colleges and professions. The 13th, 14th, and 15th Amendments to the Constitution promised equal rights to all, but these had been reversed by state actions. In the South, African Americans had no right to vote, hold office, serve on juries, or have equal access to public accommodations. They were segregated in theaters, trains, and government buildings.

In 1896, in the Plessy case, the Supreme Court ruled that segregation was not discrimination and did not violate the Constitution. It stated that equal facilities had to be provided for each race, but everyone knew African Americans would never be given equal facilities with whites. For the next 58 years, this Supreme Court ruling made segregation legal and normal in the North and South.

Despite segregation laws in the South, some African Americans were elected to Congress and local offices. In 1890, 16 black legislators served in the Louisiana legislature. In 1899, voters in Liberty County, Georgia, elected two African Americans to the state legislature. Between 1870 and 1899, 22 African Americans were elected to the U.S. Congress.

In this age of lynching, some African American figures insisted that terror and violence had to be stopped no matter the cost. In

Dissenting Voice

Henry McNeal Turner, the first African American chaplain in the Civil War, entered politics during Reconstruction. He and 26 other blacks were elected to the Georgia legislature but then were expelled by the white majority. It was an event he did not forget.

In 1880, Turner became one of 12 Bishops of the African Methodist Episcopal Church. He always tried to promote self-help and build pride among his people. He once said, "God is a Negro."

He thought that white Americans were hopelessly racist and came to this conclusion, "There is no manhood future in the United States for the Negro. He may eke out an existence for generations to come, but he can never be a man full, symmetrical, and undwarfed."

Turner believed his people should migrate to Africa, the ancestral homeland. He traveled to Africa a total of four times searching for suitable sites for African American colonies. He finally left the United States for Canada and died in 1915 in Ontario. ∎

The Voice of Moderation

The outstanding African American figure of the late 19th and early 20th centuries was Booker T. Washington, a former slave whose life seemed to prove that anyone with determination and a decent education could succeed in America. As the first president of the Tuskegee Institute, he taught his students to learn trades and practice self-reliance.

In 1895, Washington delivered a speech at the Atlanta Exposition that gave him instant fame. He told his people that "social equality is the extremist folly" and urged them to accept segregation. His "Atlanta compromise" was a message to his people to work hard, not take part in strikes, and try to win bigoted whites to their side.

President Grover Cleveland wrote Washington a letter of praise and leading whites applauded his views as reasonable and progressive. Millionaires Andrew Carnegie and John D. Rockefeller provided funds for Washington for black industrial education. He became a consultant to U.S. Presidents on the appointments of African Americans, and sometimes whites, to federal jobs in the South.

Washington tried to bridge the gap between his people and the white bastions of power. In an age when racial hatred was written into law, he said, "When your head is in the lion's mouth, use your hand to pet him." Black people hoped that Washington's power would provide them protection and benefits from white society.

Washington's "Atlanta compromise" was soon challenged by other African American leaders who insisted the fight for full equality could not be traded away. "I want equality, nothing else," said President John Hope of Atlanta University. Some scoffed that Washington himself did not really believe what he had said.

Washington emphasized learning a trade at a time when modern industry was rapidly eliminating any need for skilled workers. He was teaching Blacks to make wheels for horse-drawn carriages when white people were turning to automobiles.

Despite pointed criticisms, Washington remained the most powerful African American in the country until his death in 1915. ■

Booker T. Washington (center) at Tuskeegee Institute, Alabama.

1889 black journalist John Bruce, known as "Bruce Grit," wrote:

> Under the present state of affairs, the only hope, the only
> salvation for the Negro, is to be found in a resort to force
> under wise and discreet leaders.

During and after the Civil War, the "Lowry Band" in North Carolina united Native Americans, African Americans, and poor whites in a guerrilla force that challenged bigoted white citizens and officials. In 1899, a thousand armed African American farmers in Georgia freed farmer Henry Delegal, who had been imprisoned for dating a white woman. Delegal and his guerrilla army hid in the Okefenokee Swamp until the Governor of Georgia agreed to settle the issue quietly and without jailing Delegal.

Boycotts against discrimination shook 30 Southern cities between 1898 and 1906. New Orleans, Mobile, and Houston lived through boycotts of streetcar lines. In Houston, Nashville, Chattanooga, and Savannah, African Americans organized their own transportation companies. These efforts dramatically challenged but did not halt racial segregation.

The "Lowry Band" operating undercover in North Carolina.

CHAPTER 21

THE PEOPLE'S PARTY

In the last decades of the 19th century many Americans felt their hopes for economic success had slipped away. A depression began in 1873 that threw tens of thousands out of work and was followed in 1893 by another one that left hundreds of thousands jobless.

Farmers were caught in a financial vice. Prices for their wheat, corn, or cotton crops fell, but the cost of seed, machinery, and rail transportation rose. When mortgages could not be paid, banks seized farms that had been owned for generations by the same families. In the South the economic squeeze caught both farm owners and sharecroppers. In the 30 years after the Civil War the price of cotton had fallen by 80 percent. Owners lost farms and sharecroppers were evicted from land they had labored on.

As discontent rose among America's farmers, they united in their own defense in organizations like the Grange and the Farmers' Alliance. The Grange charged that wealthy railroad owners, eastern bankers, and owners of monopolies threatened the economic survival of farmers. Ordinary people, said the farmers, had to unite to save democracy from a rich elite. They feared that a wealthy few were gaining complete control of the government.

Women played a vital part in the Farmers Alliances of the 1880s. An observer noted, "Women with skins tanned to parchment by the hot winds, with bony hands of toil and clad in faded calico, could talk in meeting, and could talk straight to the point."

The agrarian protest in the South was divided by race. Since the Southern Farmers' Alliance did not admit African Americans, black farmers formed a Colored Farmers National Alliance (CFNA). By 1891 the CFNA boasted more than a million members in 12 states.

By 1892 the farmers' alliances became the basis of the new People's Party, or Populists. Minorities played a leading role in the Populist movement. A German American labor union in Missouri took a key role in starting their state's party. In New Mexico, Mexican Americans in San Miguel County became the backbone of the local Populists. In Minnesota, French Canadian immigrant laborers and their sons formed a Populist club.

Mary Ellen Lease, called Mary "Yellin" Lease because of her flamboyant oratory, was a leading Populist speaker. The daughter of Irish political refugees, she first won public acclaim for brilliant lectures on Ireland. After Lease earned a law degree, she toured the Middle West for the party telling farmers to "raise less corn and more hell." She advocated such reforms as women's suffrage, direct election of Senators, government control of railroads, and supervision of corporations.

Mrs. Mary Ellen Lease was one of the Populist Party's most powerful speakers.

The party's most original political thinker, Ignatius Donnelly, was born to Irish immigrants. In 1863 he became the new state of Minnesota's first lieutenant governor, and then served three terms in Congress.

At its 1892 presidential convention Donnelly wrote the Populist Party platform, urging American voters to retake America from the wealthy elite and corporations. Farmers and city workers, said Donnelly, must unite to save democracy in the United States.

Some of the Populists' most enthusiastic supporters were African Americans in the South. They saw the party as their vehicle to overturn segregation and the Democrats' one-party control of the South. In Georgia and North Carolina in particular black voters played a leading role in the party. When the Populist presidential candidate, James Weaver, rode into Raleigh, North Carolina, in 1892, 350 African Americans and white horsemen led the parade.

In 1892 Weaver polled over a million votes and won 22 electoral votes. The Populist Party elected ten Representatives and five Senators to the U.S. Congress. The party also won hundreds of state offices and gained many new supporters.

In 1894 Laurence Gronlund, a Danish immigrant and editor, called on labor unions to join the party. A Populist Women's Auxiliary was formed to aid the party in Chicago. In 1894 Donnelly campaigned alongside Eugene Debs, a son of Alsatian immigrants and the popular president of the American Railway Union.

Eugene Debs

In 1894 the Populist vote soared by 50 percent. It elected six Senators and six Congressmen and hundreds of local officials. Some

22 Populists sat in the Texas legislature. The party's vote rose significantly in major cities. San Francisco had a Populist mayor.

As the Presidential election of 1896 approached, the man most often mentioned as the Populist candidate was Debs. Though a majority in 22 state delegations favored the labor leader, Debs withdrew his name, saying his nomination might divide the party.

The Democratic Party nominated William Jennings Bryan and adopted many Populist slogans. The Populists then decided to support Bryan and the Democrats. But African American voters in the South saw this as betrayal since the Democratic Party ran for the South's system of white supremacy. To show their resentment, African American Populists urged a vote for the vice presidential candidacy of Populist Tom Watson.

The 1896 election became a turning point in American history. To defeat Bryan, the Republican Party solicited huge contributions from corporations and wealthy individuals. This cash financed a massive propaganda campaign to warn voters of Bryan's radical (Populist) ideas. Republican presidential candidate William McKinley won the election by promising labor "a full dinner pail."

The People's Party had embraced and opened political gates for minorities. For example, Populist Andrew Lee became the first Norwegian American Governor of South Dakota. When Populists strongly appealed to minorities, the two older parties realized that elections could be won and lost on minority votes. By 1898 the Republican Party nominated and elected John Lind as Minnesota's first Swedish American governor.

In North Carolina, in 1896, ex-slave George Henry White, of African and Native American ancestry, was elected to Congress by a Republican-Populist coalition. In 1898, despite massive violence against black voters, he was reelected to a second term.

As the lone African American voice in Congress, White spoke for "the life, the liberty, the future happiness, and manhood suffrage of one-eighth of the entire population of the United States." He warned Congress of American racism:

> You have got this problem to settle, and the sooner it is
> settled the better it will be for all concerned. I speak this in
> all charity. I speak this with no hostility.

Further Reading

Adamic, Louis. *A Nation of Nations*. New York: Harper, 1944.

The Council on Interracial Books for Children, ed. *Chronicles of American Indian Protest*. Greenwich, CT: Fawcett Publications, 1971.

Johns, Stephanie Bernado. *The Ethnic Almanac*. Garden City, NY: Doubleday, 1981.

Debo, Angie. *A History of the Indians of the United States*, rev. ed. Norman, OK: University of Oklahoma Press, 1984.

The Ethnic Chronology Series. Dobbs Ferry, NY: Oceana Publications, 1972-1990.

Evans, Sara M. *Born for Liberty: A History of Women in America*. New York: Macmillan, 1989.

Franklin, John Hope. *From Slavery to Freedom: A History of Negro Americans*, rev. ed. New York: Alfred A. Knopf, 1988.

Handlin, Oscar. *The Uprooted; The Epic Story of the Great Migrations that Made the American People*. New York: Grosset & Dunlap, 1951.

Katz, William Loren. *Black Indians: A Hidden Heritage*. New York: Atheneum Publishers, 1986.

———— *Breaking the Chains: African American Slave Resistance*. New York: Atheneum Publishers, 1990.

Millstein, Beth and Bodin, Jeanne, eds. *We, The American Women: A Documentary History*. Englewood, NJ: Ozer Publishing, 1977.

Moquin, Wayne, ed. *A Documentary History of the Mexican Americans*. New York: Praeger, 1972.

Schlissel, Lillian. *Women's Diaries of the Westward Journey*. New York: Schocken Books, 1982.

Seller, Maxine S. *To Seek America: A History of Ethnic Life in the United States*. Englewood, NJ: Ozer Publishing, 1977.

Shannon, William V. *The American Irish*. New York: Macmillan, 1964.

Thernstrom, Stephan, ed. *Harvard Encyclopedia of American Ethnic Groups*. Cambridge, MA: Belknap, 1980.

INDEX